MW01097761

Intuit QuickBooks Enterprise Edition 12.0 Cookbook for Experts

60 plus recipes to save time and increase effectiveness in data entry, supervision, and business management for both public and industry accountants

Jaime Campbell, CPA, MBA, CTT, MCT

[PACKT] enterprise
PUBLISHING   professional expertise distilled

BIRMINGHAM - MUMBAI

Intuit QuickBooks Enterprise Edition 12.0 Cookbook for Experts

Copyright © 2012 Packt Publishing

All rights reserved. No part of this book may be reproduced, stored in a retrieval system, or transmitted in any form or by any means, without the prior written permission of the publisher, except in the case of brief quotations embedded in critical articles or reviews.

Every effort has been made in the preparation of this book to ensure the accuracy of the information presented. However, the information contained in this book is sold without warranty, either express or implied. Neither the author, nor Packt Publishing, and its dealers and distributors will be held liable for any damages caused or alleged to be caused directly or indirectly by this book.

Packt Publishing has endeavored to provide trademark information about all of the companies and products mentioned in this book by the appropriate use of capitals. However, Packt Publishing cannot guarantee the accuracy of this information.

First published: May 2012

Production Reference: 1230412

Published by Packt Publishing Ltd.
Livery Place
35 Livery Street
Birmingham B3 2PB, UK.

ISBN 978-1-84968-514-6

www.packtpub.com

Cover Image by Mark Holland (MJH767@bham.ac.uk)

Credits

Author
Jaime Campbell
(CPA, MBA, CTT, MCT)

Reviewers
Cheryl A Bergen
Susan R Banziger

Acquisition Editor
Dhwani Devater

Lead Technical Editor
Shreerang Deshpande

Technical Editors
Lubna Shaikh
Ameya Sawant

Copy Editor
Brandt D'mello
Laxmi Subhramanian

Project Coordinator
Michelle Quadros

Proofreader
Joanna McMahon

Indexer
Monica Ajmera Mehta

Graphics
Manu Joseph
Valentina D'silva

Production Coordinator
Alwin Roy

Cover Work
Alwin Roy

About the Author

Jaime Campbell, CPA, MBA, CTT, MCT

As a young musician, Jaime learned that mastery brings freedom and possibility. As she studied her piano repertoire, she ascertained that if she learned how to play the music as the composer intended, then she could invent new ways to play it.

As a music education student at Florida State University, learning to play instruments from South America, China, Bali, and Ghana as well as many different vocal styles from around the world, Jaime understood that deep expertise, as a gateway to self-expression, must be a given. In other words, there's more fun to be had when you can play the notes correctly the first time – than spend your time experimenting and creating instead of just learning the notes!

As a music teacher, Jaime created some special ensembles, one of which was rehearsing before school one day. The children knew the music very well, and Jaime had them play it by clapping… then on drums… then they went outside and played the same music with sticks upon the metal fence. Suddenly one student exclaimed:

"Oh!" he said, "I get it! The music isn't inside the instrument – it's inside of me!"

Now a Certified Public Accountant with a Master of Business Administration degree from Rutgers Business School, Jaime still believes that mastery brings freedom and possibility. Her foray into business computing started with the F1 key (Help) and she soon mastered the software essential to her trade, becoming a Certified QuickBooks Professional Advisor and a Certified Microsoft Master.

Propelled by a desire to help other businesspeople to transform their experience of software from one of drudgery to one of opportunity, she attained additional designations of Certified Technical Trainer and Microsoft Certified Trainer. Jaime now delivers seminars, webinars and workshops, and provides technology consulting services.

Jaime wrote this book as an expression of her sense of discovery and play, of moving quickly through mundane tasks and into the complex, value-added areas to help businesses gain significant, actionable insights.

Jaime is a member of the **American Institute for Certified Public Accountants (AICPA)** and the **New Jersey Society of Certified Public Accountants (NJSCPA)**. She is also a member of the NJSCPA Technology Interest Group and Financial Literacy Interest Group, serves as an Officer on the NJSCPA Mercer County Chapter Board of Directors, is a member of the **New Jersey Association for Women Business Owners (NJAWBO)**, and volunteers as a Spanish-language business consultant with the New Jersey Small Business Development Center.

After all these years of teaching and working personally with business owners and their teams, this book was a great deal of fun to write. The writing process felt just like giving a workshop for a sold-out house!

Jaime wishes each reader freedom and possibility with QuickBooks.

Jaime welcomes connections on social media to discuss matters of accounting, business, and technology:

www.linkedin.com/in/jcampbellcpa

www.facebook.com/jcampbellcpa

www.twitter.com/#!/jcampbellcpa

Acknowledgment

Thank you, David Campbell, for being my partner in inventing new realms of possibility. www.tieroneservices.net

Thank you, Trisha Scudder, for helping me to see an abundance of opportunity and miracles, and for teaching me to be the cause of more of both. www.executivecoachgroup.com

Thank you, Bob Lissau, for providing my first experience with QuickBooks, and for helping me to become a fun-loving, puzzle-solving CPA.

Thank you, Loni Kalver, for your love, talent, and kvelling.

Thank you, Karen Hodges Miller, for igniting the spark of the idea to be an author. www.opendoorpublications.com

Thank you, Cheryl Bergen, for being a fellow QuickBooks geek and proud of it. www.bergenbookkeeping.com

Thank you, Susan Banzinger, for being a stand for high-quality processes and results. www.yourbottomlinellc.com

Thank you, Dr. Robyn Odegaard, for your powerful words and coaching, your fun friendship, and for sharing the experience of being an author. www.StopTheDramaNow.com, www.champperformance.com

Gracias, Ernesto y Dora Lyd Robayo, por su apoyo, su amistad, su amor, su risa, y su inspiración.

Thank you, Jackie Lawrence, for telling me in that NYC coffee shop that I would one day publish a book, and you asked me to promise to mention you on this page!

Thank you, Packt team, for your expertise, professionalism, and integrity at every stage in the publishing process.

About the Reviewers

Cheryl A Bergen is an Intuit Certified QuickBooks ProAdvisor®, and has been using Intuit products since the 1980s. She has written and developed computer programs from concept to ongoing operation, written user manuals, and trained people in a multitude of programs.

Cheryl specializes in full-charge bookkeeping services for small businesses. She is extremely qualified with the QuickBooks accounting software. She assists clients in effectively utilizing it in their own businesses, and by providing bookkeeping, sales tax, and payroll services for them. She also helps businesses with a wide range of QuickBooks-related services including installation, configuration, training, and advanced uses of the software.

Susan R Banziger received a Bachelor of Science degree from Rutgers University in 1985. She has over 25 years of accounting experience in corporate and small business. She has worked in the service and manufacturing industries, in general and cost accounting. Her last position before opening her own company was as a Divisional Controller for a large specialty printing company, which included traveling with an investment team setting up scratch-off lottery programs in Europe.

After leaving the corporate world, Ms. Banziger opened Your Bottom Line, LLC. Your Bottom Line, LLC offers Certified Bookkeepers and Certified QuickBooks ProAdvisors to small business clients in the New Jersey area.

Ms. Banziger resides in New Jersey with her husband of 29 years and her two sons.

She would like to thank the author, Jaime Campbell, for the incredible opportunity of working with her, and Packt Publishing in bringing this book to the market.

www.PacktPub.com

Support files, eBooks, discount offers and more

You might want to visit www.PacktPub.com for support files and downloads related to your book.

Did you know that Packt offers eBook versions of every book published, with PDF and ePub files available? You can upgrade to the eBook version at www.PacktPub.com and as a print book customer, you are entitled to a discount on the eBook copy. Get in touch with us at service@packtpub.com for more details.

At www.PacktPub.com, you can also read a collection of free technical articles, sign up for a range of free newsletters and receive exclusive discounts and offers on Packt books and eBooks.

http://PacktLib.PacktPub.com

Do you need instant solutions to your IT questions? PacktLib is Packt's online digital book library. Here, you can access, read and search across Packt's entire library of books.

Why Subscribe?

- ▶ Fully searchable across every book published by Packt
- ▶ Copy and paste, print and bookmark content
- ▶ On demand and accessible via web browser

Free Access for Packt account holders

If you have an account with Packt at www.PacktPub.com, you can use this to access PacktLib today and view nine entirely free books. Simply use your login credentials for immediate access.

Instant Updates on New Packt Books

Get notified! Find out when new books are published by following @PacktEnterprise on Twitter, or the *Packt Enterprise* Facebook page.

Table of Contents

Preface

Intuit QuickBooks Enterprise Edition 12.0 is an accounting software that is both user-friendly and sophisticated. The interface is not only visual and intuitive, but also feature-rich for mid-size businesses, as well as complex, growing small businesses.

Intuit QuickBooks Enterprise Edition 12.0 for Experts is a cookbook with specific recipes for time-saving shortcuts, valuable customized reports, and surprising ways to use this accounting software to support decision-making in your small or medium-sized business.

With *Intuit QuickBooks Enterprise Edition 12.0 Cookbook for Experts*, you can choose a topic of value, and learn specific and practical techniques usable in your own QuickBooks file or in a sample file.

You will:

- ▶ Become agile with keyboard shortcuts and time-saving techniques, which are most valuable to practitioners
- ▶ Be a hero with troubleshooting tips and error-finding methods
- ▶ Learn the latest features available in this edition, whether you're upgrading from Premier, or from a prior version of Enterprise edition
- ▶ Learn new techniques for achieving standard and unconventional results with QuickBooks

What this book covers

Chapter 1, Special Capabilities of the Enterprise Edition. You will gain access to often-overlooked features and capabilities not available in other versions of QuickBooks, including user permissions and ODBC-based reports.

Chapter 2, Customizing the Interface. You will create a more comfortable QuickBooks environment for your working style by eliminating interruptions to the thought process and making the most relevant information more accessible, thereby speeding up daily processes and accelerating results.

Chapter 3, Items. You will use items strategically to accelerate workflow, reduce errors, increase accuracy of your accounting records, and extract critical accounting information from your QuickBooks files.

Chapter 4, Special Tools. You will smoothly navigate through linked transactions, quickly views the General Ledger effect of a transaction, and efficiently locates transactions and other relevant information.

Chapter 5, Customizing Reports. You will create meaningful reports beyond those which are readily available in the QuickBooks Report Center. You will learn to adeptly preserve and organize highly customized reports.

Chapter 6, Memorized Transactions. You will eliminate and redude the data entry time, and increase the accuracy of repetitive transactions. You will learn how to keep these shortcuts organized and accessible.

Chapter 7, Customer and Vendor Relations. You will utilize non-accounting information to manage relationships with customers and vendors. These recipes include communication, management tools, and customizations of customer and vendor records.

Chapter 8, Troubleshooting. You will examine a number of accounting errors that are common in QuickBooks files, and enables you to be powerful and efficient in resolving them.

Chapter 9, Keyboard Shortcuts. You will dramatically increase the speed of those QuickBooks tasks that are most important and common to you. Use the relevant shortcuts included in these recipes, but transfer the underlying techniques to other areas of QuickBooks to suit your working style.

Chapter 10, Integration with Excel. You will use advanced integration features with Microsoft Excel, including preparing combined reports from multiple QuickBooks files, setting up reports for optimal analysis once exported into Excel, and moving information from Excel into QuickBooks.

Chapter 11, Supervisory Tools. As a supervisor or reviewer, you will locate and address incorrect entries and inconsistencies in the accounting records by using the latest tools, as well as by using old tools in new ways.

Chapter 12, New for the 12.0 Edition. You will gain access to the features and capabilities that were not available in previous versions of the QuickBooks Enterprise edition.

What you need for this book

To run the examples in the book the following software will be required:

▶ QuickBooks: Enterprise edition

Most of the recipes in the book are also useful for the Pro or Premier versions. Furthermore, most of the recipes in the book are useful for many editions prior to the 12.0 edition.

Most of the recipes are useful for any industry edition, and a few are available only in the Accountant edition. These are mentioned specifically in the book.

▶ Excel: Microsoft Excel 2007 or 2010

Who this book is for

This book is written for CPAs, CAs, consultants, CFOs, controllers, managers, or bookkeepers with extensive experience with QuickBooks. Prior experience with the Enterprise edition, however, is not required. You should have a thorough understanding of accounting procedures and a mastery of the basics of the QuickBooks environment.

Conventions

In this book, you will find a number of styles of text that distinguish between different kinds of information. Here are some examples of these styles, and an explanation of their meaning.

Code words in text are shown as follows: "Manage product mix and pricing using the `Sales by Item Summary` option as follows:."

New terms and important words are shown in bold. Words that you see on the screen, in menus or dialog boxes for example, appear in the text like this: "Instead of clicking on **New**, as you did when adding new users, click on the **Role List** tab."

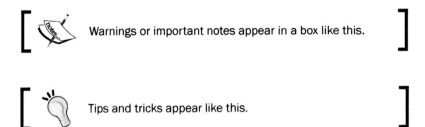

Warnings or important notes appear in a box like this.

Tips and tricks appear like this.

Reader feedback

Feedback from our readers is always welcome. Let us know what you think about this book—what you liked or may have disliked. Reader feedback is important for us to develop titles that you really get the most out of.

To send us general feedback, simply send an e-mail to feedback@packtpub.com, and mention the book title through the subject of your message.

If there is a topic that you have expertise in and you are interested in either writing or contributing to a book, see our author guide on www.packtpub.com/authors.

Customer support

Now that you are the proud owner of a Packt book, we have a number of things to help you to get the most from your purchase.

Errata

Although we have taken every care to ensure the accuracy of our content, mistakes do happen. If you find a mistake in one of our books—maybe a mistake in the text or the code—we would be grateful if you would report this to us. By doing so, you can save other readers from frustration and help us improve subsequent versions of this book. If you find any errata, please report them by visiting http://www.packtpub.com/support, selecting your book, clicking on the **errata submission form** link, and entering the details of your errata. Once your errata are verified, your submission will be accepted and the errata will be uploaded to our website, or added to any list of existing errata, under the Errata section of that title.

Piracy

Piracy of copyright material on the Internet is an ongoing problem across all media. At Packt, we take the protection of our copyright and licenses very seriously. If you come across any illegal copies of our works, in any form, on the Internet, please provide us with the location address or website name immediately so that we can pursue a remedy.

Please contact us at `copyright@packtpub.com` with a link to the suspected pirated material.

We appreciate your help in protecting our authors, and our ability to bring you valuable content.

Questions

You can contact us at `questions@packtpub.com` if you are having a problem with any aspect of the book, and we will do our best to address it.

1
Special Capabilities of the Enterprise Edition

In this chapter, we will cover the following recipes:

- ▸ Customizing user permissions
- ▸ Creating highly-customized reports with ODBC
- ▸ Using the Employee Organizer

Introduction

You will be able to use the recipes in this chapter to gain access to the often-overlooked features and capabilities that are not available in other versions of QuickBooks. Recipes for a number of features, only available in the Enterprise edition, are also included throughout this cookbook.

Customizing user permissions

As compared to the **Premier** and **Pro** editions, user permissions in the Enterprise edition are much more detailed and specific. Furthermore, the role-based structure of **user permissions** allows the administrator to automate the process after the initial setup.

Getting ready

Make sure that all bank accounts that are going to be used by the company have been added to the Chart of Accounts. There are certain permissions, which are bank account-specific.

How to do it...

1. Go to **Company | Users | Set Up Users and Roles**.

2. Instead of clicking on **New**, as you did when adding new users, click on the **Role List** tab.

3. Click on **New**, **Edit**, or **Duplicate** to start working with a role that you wish to customize.

4. Depending on your choice in the previous step, the following pop-up box is prepared already or completely blank, as in the following illustration:

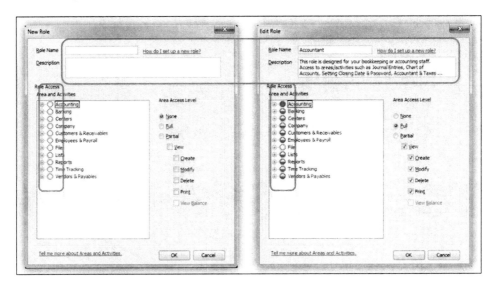

5. Edit or create the **Role Name**.

6. Use the **Description** field to detail either the type of position suitable for that user role, or the types of permissions included in this user role.

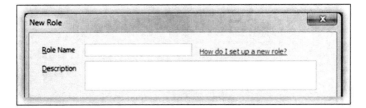

7. In the **Role Access | Area and Activities** section, select the **+** to the left of an area of interest to you.

8. Select an activity.

9. From the **Activity Access Level** section, make your selection as to the extent of the access level. Depending on the activity, the choices are **None/Full**:

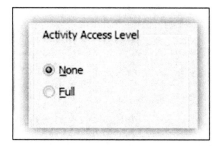

Or **None/Full/Partial**, followed by additional options for **Partial**:

10. If you select **Partial**, select the additional checkboxes according to the access you wish to grant for this specific activity in this specific role.

11. Click on **OK** to complete the process.

There's more...

From the **Users and Roles** dialog box displayed, after you click on **Company | Users | Set Up Users and Roles**, the **User List** tab includes a display for the roles assigned to the selected user.

Similarly, the **Role List** tab includes a display for the users assigned to the selected role.

 For a quick overview of all of the permissions for a specific user or for a specific role, select the **View Permissions** button. Check off your desired user or role, and click on the **Display** button.

Creating highly-customized reports with ODBC

This cookbook includes many recipes for customized reports, including modifying standard reports in QuickBooks, and using the QuickBooks Statement Writer. The **Open Database Connectivity (ODBC)** feature, available exclusively in the Enterprise edition, provides access to further customization of reports. This recipe details ODBC with Microsoft Excel 2007 or 2010, but the connection is possible with Microsoft Access as well.

Getting ready

Your file must be in a **multi-user** mode in order to use the ODBC feature. Even if you have a single-user license, you can still access the multi-user mode for this purpose, by clicking **File | Switch to Multi-User Mode**.

Additionally, you need to know the location of your QuickBooks file. An easy way to get this information is to open your QuickBooks file, and press the *F2* key. The middle of the dialog box has a section called **File Information**, which contains the location:

File Information
Location C:\Users\Public\Documents\Intuit\QuickBooks\Sample
Company Files\QuickBooks Enterprise Solutions
12.0\sample_manufacturing business.QBW

How to do it...

1. Go to **Reports | Custom Reporting**.

2. The first time you use the ODBC feature, click on the **Manage ODBC Users** button to create an ODBC user.

3. Click on the **New** button.

4. Create a username and password. The following red message turns green when a password with at least six characters is entered.

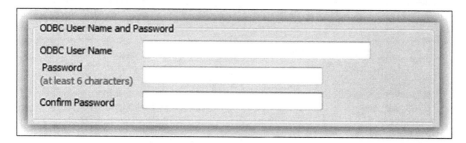

5. Click on any number of groups from the left-hand side of the dialog box:

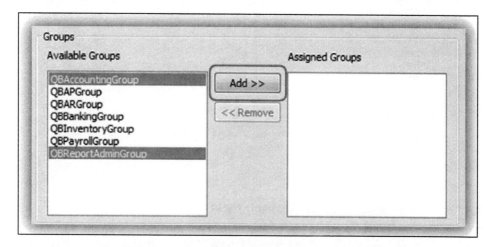

6. Click on the **Add** button, followed by **OK** and **Close**.

7. Open Microsoft Excel.

8. Go to **Data | From Other Sources | From Microsoft Query | Databases | Browse**.

9. Browse to the folder containing your QuickBooks file, and double-click on the appropriate file.

10. Click on **OK**.

11. Fill out the **User ID** and **Password** fields using the same information you entered earlier in this recipe.

12. Go to **Options | In the Creator** drop-down box, select **QBReportAdminGroup | OK**.

13. Select a desired table, and click on the **>** button. For just a single field, click on the **+** button, and select a single field, followed by the **>** button.

14. Click on **Next**.

15. If necessary, establish a join between the tables in the query. In the following example, the v_lst_customer (**Customer List**) and v_lst_customer_type (**Customer Type List**) fields were added to the query. The join in the illustration was created by dragging the id field to the customer_type_id field:

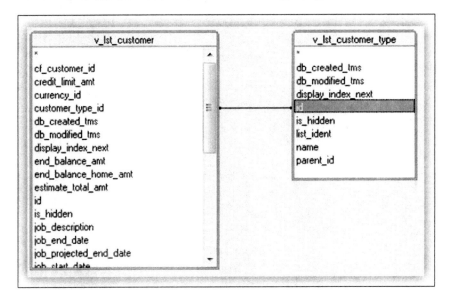

16. Sort and filter as desired.

17. Select **File | Save**.

18. Select **File | Return Data to Microsoft Excel**.

19. Use the **Import Data** dialog box to determine how you wish to see the information in Excel. If you wish to see details, click on **Table**. For a summary, click on **PivotTable**. For a visual summary, click on **PivotChart** and **PivotTable** report:

20. Manipulate the information as you would in any Excel spreadsheet, and interpret the information.

There's more...

The ODBC feature can be used to get key information, which is not otherwise readily available in QuickBooks. For example, you can obtain your customer Accounts Receivable balances by state, in order to focus your collection efforts in a particular geographic region:

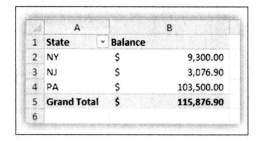

Also noteworthy is that for transactions and reports, the relationship between QuickBooks and Excel is one-way. That is, information can be exported from QuickBooks to Excel, but neither custom reports nor transaction information can be moved from Excel back into QuickBooks.

Using the Employee Organizer

The Employee Organizer goes beyond the Employee Center in the administration of the human resource function. It focuses on employment processes, includes regulations guides, and provides access to additional resources, such as background checks. The Enterprise edition's array of employee reports also includes special reports that are not offered in other versions of QuickBooks. This recipe details the use of the task-based items of employment processes and special reports.

Getting ready

Be sure that your employees are included in the **Employee List**.

Open the Employee Organizer by selecting **Employees | Employee Organizer | Employee Organizer Home**.

How to do it...

Employment processes:

1. Use the links given in the following screenshot to gain access to different processes and resources:

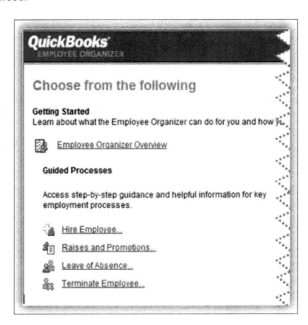

2. Click on the **Hire Employee** link to view resources. Click on **payroll items** to jump to the **Payroll Item List**, to add items to the list if needed.

3. Click on the **Raises and Promotions** link to adjust the employee's hourly rate, title, or relevant payroll item.

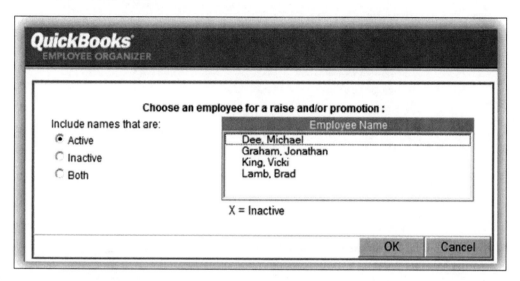

4. Select the appropriate employee, and click on **OK**.

5. Use the **Enter Raise or Promotion** button or the **Add Historical Record** button to indicate the following changes:

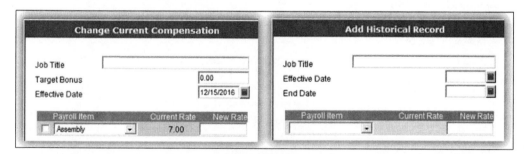

6. Click on **OK**. If desired, click on the **Report** button for an employee compensation history report, for the selected employee.

7. Click on the **Leave of Absence** link to start the wizard regarding the leave. Options include considerations for the Family Leave Act, USERRA, disability-related leave, and paid leave.

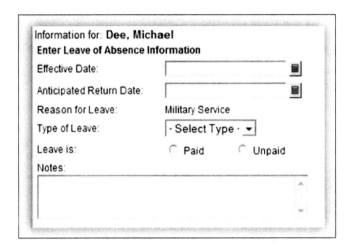

8. Click on the **Terminate Employee** link to start the related wizard. Options include the reason for the termination, recommendations to re-hire, and severance. Some information from the wizard affects the payroll reports, such as whether the employee is deceased, which will be indicated on the employee's annual earnings report.

Reports

1. Go to **Reports | Employees and Payroll**.

2. The list includes several reports that are not included in other versions of QuickBooks:

2
Customizing the Interface

In this chapter, we will cover:

- ► Customizing the icon bar
- ► Customizing the home page
- ► Customizing QuickBooks windows
- ► Shortening the data entry process for customer payments

Introduction

This chapter contains the recipes useful in creating a more comfortable **QuickBooks** environment for the working style of the reader by eliminating interruptions to the thought process, and making the most relevant information more accessible, thereby speeding up daily processes and accelerating results.

The following table is the **Recipe Reference Card** for the keyboard shortcuts included in this chapter:

Chart of Accounts	Ctrl+A
New account	Ctrl+N

Customizing the icon bar

With this recipe, you will be able to remove unnecessary and low-priority buttons from your **icon bar**. Instead, add shortcut buttons for your own high-frequency data entry screens and reports. Although the ultimate goal is to use this personalized area to save time in the ongoing data entry, analysis, and reporting, a customized icon bar may also be used to provide a logical sequence of steps for a new member of your accounting team.

Getting ready

First, clear the icon bar of unwanted icons as follows:

1. Select **View | Customize Icon Bar**.
2. Select the unwanted **item.**
3. Click on **Delete**.
4. Repeat steps 2 and 3 until all unwanted icons are deleted. Click on **OK**.

How to do it...

1. Use conventional means to bring up your favorite data entry screen or report.
2. Select **View | Add** to add the name of the screen or the report to the icon bar.
3. Select your desired icon and type your desired label and description. Click on **OK**. The **Label** text shows up beneath the icon. The **Description** text appears as a tool tip upon mouse hover, as shown in the following screenshot:

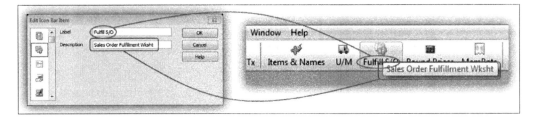

There's more...

To edit an existing icon or to change the label or description, perform the following steps:

1. Select **View | Customize Icon Bar**.
2. Select the desired item.
3. Click on **Edit**, make changes.

4. Click on **OK** again to close the **Customize Icon Bar** box.

To rearrange the order of the icons on the icon bar, perform the following steps:

1. Select **View | Customize Icon Bar**.
2. Select the diamond next to the item you want to move.
3. Drag the diamond to the desired position.
4. Click on **OK** as shown in the following screenshot:

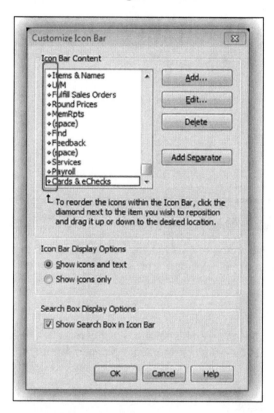

Right-click anywhere on the icon bar to display the **Customize Icon Bar** choice.

To add a vertical separator to the icon bar in order to separate the icons into logical groupings, open the **Customize Icon Bar** box and click on **Add Separator**. The separator appears in the **Icon Bar Content** list as **(space)**.

As indicated in the preceding illustration, the **Search Box** on the icon bar can be toggled on and off from the **Customize Icon Bar** box. It is also available in the **View** menu, as shown in the following screenshot:

Customizing the home page

You will be able to use this recipe only to include icons on your home page which are relevant to your business, eliminating visual clutter and inappropriate data entry choices.

Getting ready

Log into the QuickBooks file as an administrator. Most companies have set up their QuickBooks files such that the administrator login is called **Admin**, and requires a specific password.

How to do it...

1. From the **Edit** menu, select **Preferences**.
2. On the top of the **Preferences** box, select the **Company Preferences** tab.
3. In the left-hand margin, select **Desktop View**.
4. Use the checkboxes to customize the home page.
5. Click on the links in the lower half of the screen to jump to other sections of the **Preferences** box with additional home page customizations.

6. After you finish, select **Desktop View** again to return to this screen, as shown in the following screenshot:

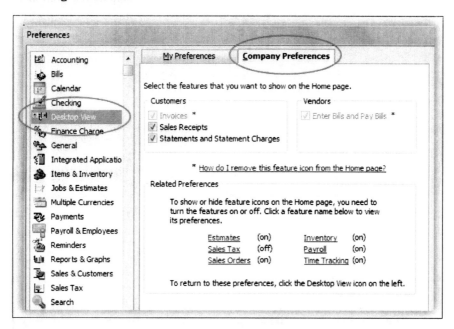

The recipe reference card for home page customizations is as follows:

Home page icon	Preferences section	Wording	Click
Invoices	Desktop View	Invoices	Checkbox
Sales receipts	Desktop View	Sales receipts	Checkbox
Statements	Desktop View	Statements and statement charges	Checkbox
Statement charges	Desktop View	Statements and statement charges	Checkbox
Sales orders	Sales and customers	Enable sales orders	Checkbox
Estimates	Jobs and estimates	Do you create estimates?	Option button
Sales tax	Sales tax	Do you charge sales tax?	Option button
Enter bills	Desktop View	Enter bills and pay bills	Checkbox
Pay bills	Desktop View	Enter bills and pay bills	Checkbox
Inventory	Items and inventory	Inventory and purchase orders are active	Checkbox
Payroll	Payroll and employees	Full payroll or no payroll	Option button
Time tracking	Time and expenses	Do you track time?	Option button

There's more...

If the banking section of your home page does not include the **Enter Credit Card Charges** button, substitute the following procedure, that is, add a credit card account to the Chart of Accounts as follows:

1. From the **Company** menu, select **Chart of Accounts** (*Ctrl+A*)

2. Select **Edit | New** (*Ctrl+N*).

3. Select **Credit Card | Continue**.

4. Name the account, and click on **Save and Close**.

Customizing QuickBooks windows

Individual users may customize the layout of the QuickBooks windows themselves. This recipe includes steps to set the default preferences for those windows as well as steps to take advantage of this feature to create a useful and surprising layout to facilitate work.

How to do it...

1. Select **Edit | Preferences | Desktop View | My Preferences**.

2. Select **Multiple Windows**, and also consider the **Desktop** group of options beneath, as shown in the following screenshot:

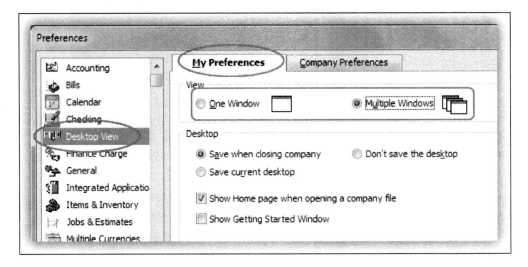

3. Click on **OK** to save your preferences, and close this window.

How it works...

You can always go to the **View** menu to toggle between **One Window** and **Multiple Windows**. However, if you constantly find yourself maximizing windows as they keep showing up as too small in the Multiple Windows, then return to **Edit | Preferences**, and change your default to **One Window**. This ensures that whenever you open a list, report, or data entry screen, it is maximized within the QuickBooks application.

There's more...

1. Open certain reports or data entry screens that you wish to visually reference simultaneously.

2. By dragging the corners and sides of these windows, you can arrange them on your screen, even arranging two reports vertically side-by-side, to simulate having multiple monitors, as shown in the following screenshot:

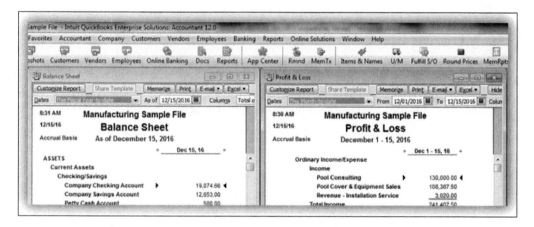

3. If you do have multiple monitors, then click on the **Restore Down** button on the QuickBooks application, stretch the application across your monitors, and then manually arrange your multiple windows as desired, as follows:

The **Save Current Desktop** option from the **Edit | Preferences** area is especially useful after arranging your commonly used reports or data entry screens in a certain formation.

The **View | Open Window List** gives you a hyperlinked left-hand margin, which always shows you the windows you have open at that time. Save time by never running reports again that you already have open.

Shortening the data entry process for customer payments

In the real world, not every customer payment is received as undeposited, and later deposited in a batch. Some may be wired directly into the bank, and some may be deposited individually. This recipe shows you how to accommodate for different scenarios, and skip over unnecessary data entry steps.

Getting ready

1. Log into the QuickBooks file as an administrator.
2. To set up the ability to skip the **Record Deposits** screen when a customer payment is deposited alone, select **Edit | Preferences | Payments | Company Preferences**.
3. Uncheck **Use Undeposited Funds as a default deposit to account**, as shown in the following screenshot:

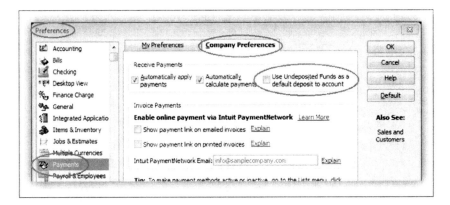

How to do it...

1. When a customer payment is deposited alone, such as a deposit slip with just one check or a payment wired directly into the checking account, skip the **Make Deposits** screen by bypassing the **Undeposited Funds** account.

2. Upon opening the **Customer Payment** screen, the **Deposit to** field will appear. Select the appropriate bank account as part of your normal data entry process. Setting this preference does not remove your ability to select **Undeposited Funds**, but expands whatever is available, as shown in the following screenshot:

3. If your business model includes upfront payments, use the same technique in the **Sales Receipt** screen, as shown in the following screenshot:

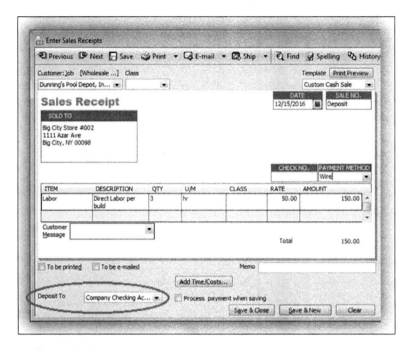

How it works...

The option to select a bank account or other current asset account for receiving customer payments becomes available when the preference to only use undeposited funds is removed.

There's more...

Caution: Changing this preference should only be done for users who have a working knowledge of the accounting process. Since this preference allows for the recording of a customer payment directly into the bank account, this option should be used with exceptional care. All deposits should still be recorded as they actually occurred, whether they are in batches, single-check deposits, or wires.

Furthermore, if the payment was received in cash, the same technique should be used, but the deposit should be recorded to a Cash on Hand account included in the Chart of Accounts as a bank account as follows:.

Receive Payments

○ If the physical payments were received and held for batch deposit, select Undeposited Funds.

○ If the payments were electronically deposited into your bank account, select the bank account.

○ For any payments received in cash, select a Cash on Hand Account

Record Deposits

○ Use the pop-up box or the Payments button to record batch deposits from Undeposited Funds.

○ When depositing cash: add a line item to the deposit, and from the From Account field, select Cash on Hand.

3
Items

In this chapter, we will cover:

- ▶ Setting up items for different purposes
- ▶ Using group items
- ▶ Configuring items for fund accounting
- ▶ Configuring inventory assembly items
- ▶ Creating standard item-based reports
- ▶ Creating customized item-based reports

Introduction

Items are required in order to use certain data screens, such as Invoices, Sales Receipts, and Purchase Orders. In other data entry screens, the optional items are Write Checks, Enter Bills, and Enter Credit Card Charges. If items are in use, it's a good idea to use them consistently throughout the accounting system to facilitate accurate reporting. By the end of this chapter, you will be able to use items strategically to accelerate workflow, reduce errors, increase accuracy of your accounting records, and extract critical accounting information from your QuickBooks files.

The following table is the **Recipe Reference Card** for the keyboard shortcuts included in this chapter:

New item	*Ctrl+N*
Edit item	*Ctrl+E*
Insert line	*Ctrl+Ins*
Delete line	*Ctrl+Del*
Transaction journal	*Ctrl+Y*

Setting up items for different purposes

With this recipe, you will be able to strategically decide which item types are most effective for different situations. You will be able to successfully create items and have them ready for use in transactions and reports.

Getting ready

From the Home page, click on the **Items & Services** icon.

How to do it...

The steps are as follows:

1. Select **Edit | New Item** (*Ctrl+N*).

2. In the **Type** drop-down box, select your item type.

3. The **Account** field, if present, is required. Other fields are generally optional and should be considered in terms of saving time by using defaults. The recipe reference card items for different purposes are as follows:

Service item	Professional fees charged or paid
Inventory Part item	Inventory purchased and sold
Inventory Assembly item	Inventory manufactured in-house
Non-inventory Part item	Materials purchased or sold which are not inventory
Other Charge item	Delivery charges or other miscellaneous fees charged or paid
Subtotal item	Automatically totals all amounts on the data entry screen between the subtotal item and the next subtotal item above it (if applicable)
Group item	Batch-enter other types of items typically purchased or sold together
Discount item	Automatically subtracts a percentage discount, or a flat amount, from the subtotal
Payment item	Partial upfront payment included in an invoice
Sales Tax item	Default sales tax rates for different taxing jurisdictions
Sales Tax	Multiple taxing jurisdictions involved in a single sale

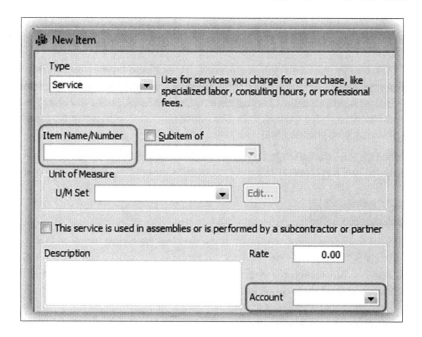

4. Select the options circled as mandatory fields, as the basic choices for the
    Service, Non-inventory part, and Other Charge item types, as shown in the
    following screenshot:

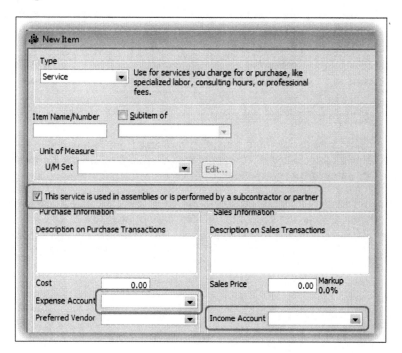

5. Whether the Service, Non-inventory Part, or Other Charge item is being created, the central checkbox circled in the previous screenshot always provides the opportunity to select a different expense account than income account to be linked to that item. Use this item in the Write Checks, Enter Bills, or Enter Credit Card Charges screen in order to have QuickBooks use the **Expense Account** selected in the preceding screenshot automatically. Use the item in the Invoices, Sales Receipts, or Credit Memo screen to have QuickBooks automatically use the **Income Account** selected in the previous screenshot.

6. Finally, use the **Job Costing** and **Item Profitability** reports described later in this chapter to pull aggregated information from transactions using these items.

There's more...

The **Discount** and **Subtotal** items work well together. The **Discount**, if used as a percentage, is automatically calculated based on the line directly preceding it in the data entry screen. If that previous line is a **Subtotal** item, then **Discount** will be calculated automatically based on **Subtotal**, as shown in the following screenshot:

ITEM	DESCRIPTION	QUANTITY	RATE	AMOUNT
Framing	Framing labor	16	55.00	880.00
Installation	Installation labor	12	35.00	420.00
Removal	Removal labor	16	35.00	560.00
Subs:Tile &Counter	Install tile or counter		825.00	825.00
Subs:Painting	Painting		154.00	154.00
Subs:Electrical	Electrical work		275.00	275.00
Subtotal	Subtotal			3,114.00
Discount	10% Discount		-10.0%	-311.40

While using items, be sure to use them consistently across transactions. For example, if you plan on using items for job costing or item profitability, be sure to use the **Items** tab, and not the **Expenses** tab, on expense transactions.

While assigning an account to items, be careful which account you select. Certain accounts, such as accounts receivable and accounts payable, cannot be linked to items. Similarly, be aware whether you are choosing profit and loss accounts, or balance sheet accounts.

Once created, certain item types may be changed by opening the **Item** list, and editing the item (*Ctrl+E*). An inventory part may be changed to inventory assembly. A non-inventory part may be changed to a service, inventory part, or an Other Charge item. An Other Charge item may be changed to a service, inventory part, or non-inventory part. You may not change other item types once the item is created and saved.

Using group items

You will be able to use this recipe to create group items, and use them in a variety of data entry screens, saving time and increasing the accuracy of your accounting records.

Getting ready

1. From the Home page, click on the **Items & Services** icon.
2. Create at least two items which are related in some way, that is, items which might appear together in the same data entry screen.

How to do it...

1. Click on **Edit | New Item** (*Ctrl+N*).
2. Enter a name for your group item. This is the name that you will ultimately select from the **Item** drop-down list on your data entry screens. The examples include items which are typically bought or sold together.
3. If you wish a default description to appear automatically on your data entry screen, enter that description in the **Description** field. Otherwise, skip this field.
4. Click on the **Item** field so that a drop-down box appears, and select items to include in your group.
5. If a default quantity is appropriate for any given item, enter it in the **Qty** field.

6. If you want the group details to show up when a document such as an invoice is printed, check the **Print items in group** checkbox. If you want the detail to be visible on the screen but not on paper, leave this box unchecked, as shown in the following screenshot:.

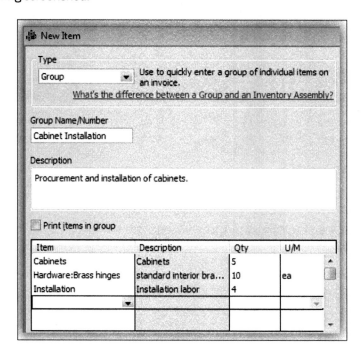

7. Once you click on **OK**, create a new invoice. Go to the **ITEM** field, and select your new group item. The component parts and default message (if applicable) appear as follows:

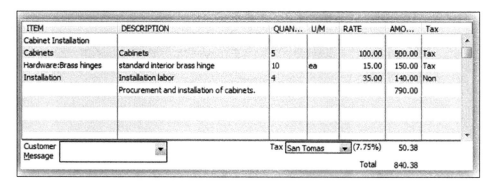

8. Since the **Print items in group** checkbox was not checked off in the preceding example, the previous invoice will print as follows:

DESCRIPTION	QUANTITY	U/M	RATE	AMOUNT
Procurement and installation of cabinets.				790.00
			Subtotal	$790.00
			Sales Tax (7.75%)	$50.38
			Total	$840.38

There's more...

Group items are ideal to speed up data entry time for items often purchased or sold together. However, you may edit the group for an unusual transaction. For example, the data entry screen in the following screenshot depicts the **Door set** group in use to record the purchase of materials. In this case, an **Interior** door needs to be added as follows:

1. Click on the line preceding the one you want to insert.
2. Click on **Edit | Insert line** (*Ctrl+Insert*).
3. Select the additional item from the drop-down box as follows:

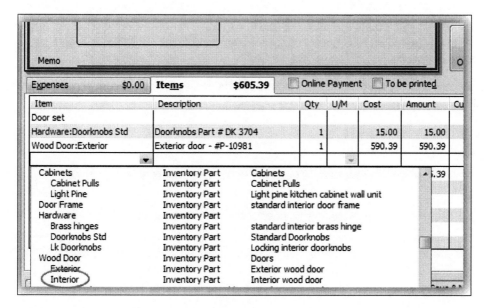

4. Similarly, use the **Edit | Delete line** command to remove single line items from a group item for one particular transaction.

Group items can be put to use in any data entry screen with an **Item** field. This includes Write Checks, Enter Bills, Enter Credit Card Charges, Purchase Orders, Sales Orders, Estimates, Invoices, Credit Memos, and Sales Receipts.

If a new combination of items becomes the norm, open the **Items** list, and edit the group item by clicking on **Edit | Edit item** or *Ctrl+E*. Changing the default contents of the group item will not change prior transactions which use that group item.

Configuring items for fund accounting

Use this novel approach to make QuickBooks work easily in a governmental or not-for-profit setting, in which certain income and expense transactions must be accompanied by a corresponding equity reclassification on the balance sheet. This recipe eliminates the need for periodic batch reclassification efforts, and provides extra transparency and readiness for external audit.

Getting ready

Make sure that your equity accounts include unrestricted funds or unrestricted net assets, as well as any restricted fund accounts such as temporarily restricted funds or temporarily restricted net assets.

The account used by QuickBooks as the default retained earnings account should be your unrestricted account.

How to do it...

Create non-taxable **Other Charge** items which mirror your equity accounts in the following way:

1. Name each item identically to its equivalent equity account.
2. If there are subaccounts in the Chart of Accounts, for example, specific donations, grants, or projects under the temporarily restricted account, create **Subitem** for these, and name them accordingly.
3. Create **Description on Purchase Transaction** and **Sales Transactions**.
4. Link each item to its corresponding equity account.

5. Give the items an amount of **1.00** as follows:

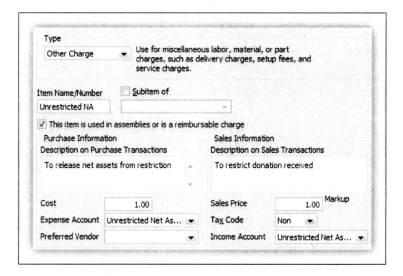

6. Create a group item. Note how the **Qty** field is used to cause QuickBooks to enter a debit and a credit to the General Ledger, as shown in the following screenshot:

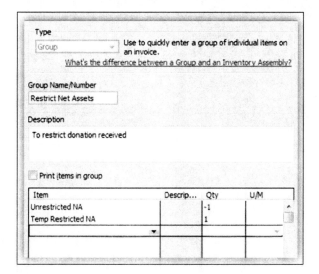

7. When a temporarily restricted donation is received, use the Sales Receipt screen to record the income and the asset restriction, as shown in the following screenshot:

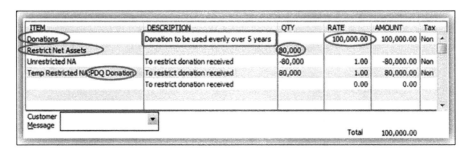

8. The circled areas in the previous screenshot indicate the only areas that need your attention during the data entry process. All other information appears automatically. Make sure you choose or create a Subitem here, if appropriate.

9. When temporarily restricted funds are released and spent as part of a designated program, use the Write Checks or Enter Bills screen as usual, but release the net assets from restriction at the same time by using your **Items** tab, as shown in the following screenshot:

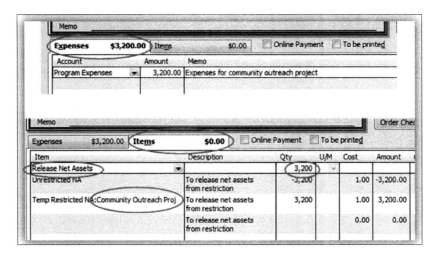

How it works...

Since the Other Charge items were created with the amount of 1, and the group item was created with inverse quantities, the result is a reclassification between equity accounts by simply using the **Qty** field. No additional journal entries are needed. Furthermore, neither the overall amount of the transaction nor the total income or expense for the period is affected by this reclassification.

There's more...

To see the journal entry underlying any data entry screen, click on the **Journal** button (*Ctrl+Y*) while that saved transaction is displayed.

Configuring inventory assembly items

Inventory Assembly items are ultra-efficient ways of recording a transformation and sale of inventory, in an assembly or manufacturing environment. Use this recipe to save time, reduce errors, and keep customer-facing documents simple and straightforward.

Getting ready

Create Inventory Part items for purchases of parts which you use in manufacturing or assembling a product, which you will sell later. For example, if you assemble and sell computers, create inventory part items for cases such as CPUs, motherboards, RAMs, graphics cards, fans, monitors, keyboards, and mouse devices.

From the Home page, click on the **Items & Services** icon.

How to do it...

1. Click on **Edit | New Item** (*Ctrl+N*).
2. In the **Type** drop-down box, select **Inventory Assembly**.

3. Fill in the mandatory fields circled in red. The other fields are optional, or are filled in automatically by QuickBooks, as shown in the following screenshot:

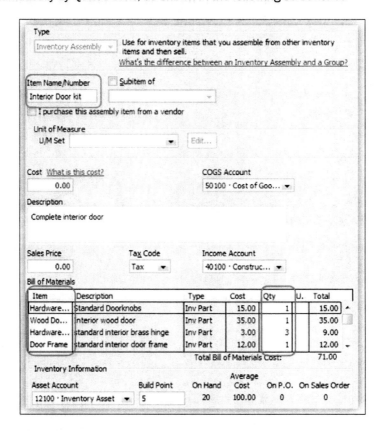

How it works...

In the Invoice or Sales Receipt screen, when an Inventory Assembly item is selected from the drop-down list and the transaction is saved, two events occur. Firstly, only that line item is visible on the screen, and not the component parts. This differs from the group item in that regard. Secondly, QuickBooks automatically subtracts each of the component parts from the inventory in terms of their quantities and valuation amounts.

There's more...

Before recording the sale of completed products, record the real-world transformation of separate component parts into completely assembled products or manufactured products. To do this, from the Home page, click on **Inventory Activities | Build Assemblies**. When you use this screen to inform QuickBooks that you have assembled five computers or manufactured 10 doors, the software makes the necessary inventory quantity adjustments.

Creating standard item-based reports

This recipe is useful for gathering valuable business intelligence from your accounting records. With these reports, you will be able to manage customer relationships, product mix and pricing, vendor relationships, and proactively plan purchases of parts and materials.

Getting ready

Use items to record purchases and/or sales. Use either Service, Inventory Part, Inventory Assembly, Non-Inventory Part, or Other Charge items for reports to be effective and powerful.

How to do it...

1. Manage customer relationships as follows:

   ❑ Click on **Reports | Jobs, Time, & Mileage | Item Estimates vs Actuals**.

   ❑ In many industries, one of the top reasons why customers leave is due to estimates, which ultimately prove to be unrealistic. Use this report to refine your estimation process while pricing a job. Click on **Customize Report** to select the following options:

   ❑ To display results only for a particular job that is similar in scope to the one which you are now estimating, go to the **Customize Report** area, and on the **Filters** tab, choose **Name** instead of **Account**. Select the job from the **Name** drop-down list, and click on **OK**.

2. Manage product mix and pricing using the Sales by Item Summary option as follows:

   ❑ Select **Reports | Sales | Sales by Item Summary**.

   ❑ This report is most useful for inventory parts, as it includes a gross margin calculation for each item. Use this information together with the sales quantities and dollar amounts to determine whether your product mix or pricing needs to be adjusted to optimize profitability.

- ❑ Click on **Customize Report** to select the following options:

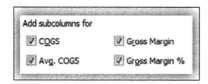

- ❑ To only display inventory items, go to the **Customize Report** area, click on the **Filters** tab, and click on **Item** in the **Choose Filter** box. Select **All Inventory Items** from the **Item** drop-down list, and click on **OK**.

3. Manage product mix and pricing using the Item Profitability option as follows:

- ❑ Select **Reports | Jobs, Time, & Mileage | Item Profitability**.
- ❑ This report is similar to the Sales by Item Summary report described previously, but it includes only dollar amounts instead of including quantities. Additionally, it includes both costs and revenues for more item types, not just inventory parts.
- ❑ For additional customizations, consider filtering by Item and select **Customize Report | Filters**. In the **Choose Filter** box, click on **Item**, then select an item type from the **Item** drop-down box, or select **Customize Report | Filters | Date**, then from the **Choose Filter** box, choose your date range to reflect the current pricing and costs.

4. Manage product mix and pricing using the Time by Item Only option as follows:

- ❑ Click on **Reports | Jobs, Time, & Mileage | Time by Item**.
- ❑ Regardless of the purchase cost of an item, labor costs should be considered when determining optimal product mix and pricing. If employees enter their labor into QuickBooks, and associate their time with Product or Service items, this report gives valuable information about the labor requirement for each item.
- ❑ Click on **Customize Report** to select the following options:

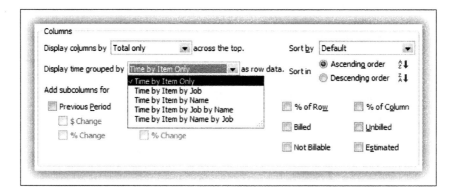

5. Manage vendor relationships as follows:

❑ Select **Reports | Customers & Receivables | Item Price List**.

❑ Select **Reports | Purchases | Purchases by Vendor Summary**.

❑ Manage risk by making sure your company is not too dependent on a small number of vendors, and negotiate with your preferred vendors by having your purchasing history and comparative cost information at your fingertips.

❑ Modify the Item Price List to show cost information by clicking on **Customize Report**, and in the **Columns** list, checking off **Cost**. Remove unnecessary columns at the same time by checking off column headers.

❑ Modify Purchases by Vendor Summary report by clicking on **Customize Report** and in the drop-down list of **Display columns**, select **Item Detail**, as shown in the following screenshot:

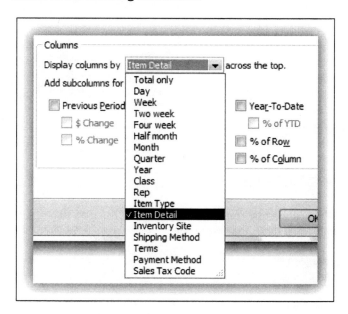

6. Plan purchases of parts and materials as follows:

    ❑ Select **Reports | Purchases | Open Purchase Orders Detail**.

    ❑ Use this report to time upcoming purchases for job completion and cashflow purposes as follows:

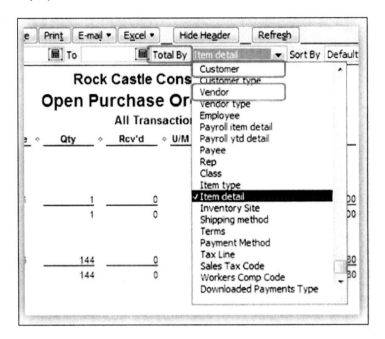

    ❑ When totaled by **Vendor**, this report can be used to place bulk orders. When totaled by **Customer**, this report can be used to place orders for priority jobs.

How it works...

Each of these reports are drawn from an Item field in the underlying data entry transactions, including Invoices, Sales Receipts, Bills, Checks, and Credit Card Charges. Since some reports require some customization to be relevant, consider memorizing the reports after you create and customize them the first time (see *Chapter 5, Customizing Reports*).

Creating customized item-based reports

Reports can be used for checking errors as well as managing operations. Item-based reports can be used in unexpected ways to highlight and fix errors in the accounting records.

Getting ready

If your company purchases certain products or services, and passes them through to the customer at cost, an Item Profitability report can be used to ensure that they pass through transactions, and are executed and recorded accurately.

When you create an item to be passed to the customer, use the fields circled in red in the following screenshot. All other fields are optional. The critical field is the **This item is used in assemblies or is a reimbursable charge** checkbox, if and only if you need purchase-type transactions, for example, Write Checks, Enter bBills, Enter Credit Card Charges, and so on, to be classified in a different General Ledger account than the income-type transactions such as Invoices, Sales Receipts, and so on:

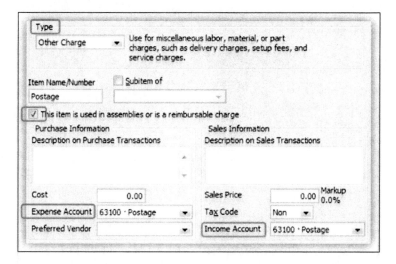

How to do it...

1. Select **Reports | Jobs, Time, & Mileage | Item Profitability**, as shown in the following screenshot:

Consulting Business
Item Profitability
All Transactions

	Act. Cost	Act. Revenue	($) Diff.
Inventory			
Books for Resale	1,674.00	3,348.00	1,674.00
Total Inventory	1,674.00	3,348.00	1,674.00
Service			
Accounting Consulting	93,314.68	105,010.00	11,695.32
Class Fee	0.00	2,100.00	2,100.00
Computer Consultant	39,530.58	94,745.00	55,214.42
Deposit	0.00	4,000.00	4,000.00
Management Consulting	23,933.73	146,500.00	122,566.27
Misc. Cables	6,461.22	5,096.70 ▶	-1,364.52 ◀
Telephone Support	40,594.86	48,910.00	8,315.14
Unbillable Time			
Meetings	86,843.18	0.00	-86,843.18
Training	16,350.00	0.00	-16,350.00
Total Unbillable Time	103,193.18	0.00	-103,193.18
Total Service	307,028.25	406,361.70	99,333.45
Other Charges			
Markup	0.00	506.85	506.85
Total Other Charges	0.00	506.85	506.85
TOTAL	308,702.25	410,216.55	101,514.30

- In the preceding report, the **Misc. Cables** item is always used for purchases which are passed through to the customer at no markup.

2. Double-click on any non-zero amount in the **($) Diff.** column to take a closer look at transactions that were not accurately passed to the customer, as shown in the following screenshot:

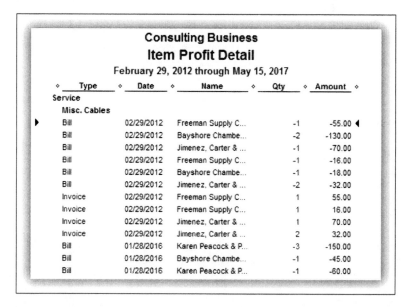

3. To quickly isolate inconsistent transactions, export to Microsoft Excel, and create a pivoted table, adding up the amounts by name, as shown in the following screenshot:

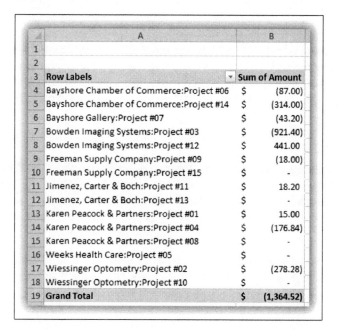

4. Now that the customers and jobs have been identified, return to QuickBooks and filter the report for the specific job with a non-zero amount by selecting **Customize Report | Filters**. Choose a name from the **Choose Filter** box, and select the job from the drop-down list as follows:

Consulting Business
Item Profit Detail
February 29, 2012 through May 15, 2017

Type	Date	Name	Amount	Balance
Service				
Misc. Cables				
Bill	01/28/2016	Bayshore Chamber of Commerce:Project #06	-45.00	-45.00
Invoice	01/31/2016	Bayshore Chamber of Commerce:Project #06	45.00	0.00
Bill	02/12/2016	Bayshore Chamber of Commerce:Project #06	-18.00	-18.00
Bill	02/28/2016	Bayshore Chamber of Commerce:Project #06	-55.00	-73.00
Invoice	02/28/2016	Bayshore Chamber of Commerce:Project #06	18.00	-55.00
Invoice	02/28/2016	Bayshore Chamber of Commerce:Project #06	55.00	0.00
Bill	03/11/2016	Bayshore Chamber of Commerce:Project #06	-18.00	-18.00
Bill	03/28/2016	Bayshore Chamber of Commerce:Project #06	-75.00	-93.00
Invoice	03/30/2016	Bayshore Chamber of Commerce:Project #06	18.00	-75.00
Invoice	03/30/2016	Bayshore Chamber of Commerce:Project #06	75.00	0.00
Bill	04/11/2016	Bayshore Chamber of Commerce:Project #06	-17.00	-17.00
Bill	04/11/2016	Bayshore Chamber of Commerce:Project #06	-15.00	-32.00
Bill	04/28/2016	Bayshore Chamber of Commerce:Project #06	-55.00	-87.00
Total Misc. Cables			-87.00	-87.00
Total Service			-87.00	-87.00
TOTAL			**-87.00**	**-87.00**

5. The preceding report illustrates the purchases and sales continued from net to zero until April 2016. At this point, expenses were incurred, but not invoiced to the customer. Take action by adding these items to the customer invoice, or take whichever other corrective action that is appropriate based on your findings.

How it works...

As an expert user, you might question why this procedure is needed if the **Time & Expenses** feature is used to efficiently invoice previous purchases. Additionally, if the **Time & Expenses** feature is used, various unbilled cost reports can track whether billable purchases were invoiced to the customer. This is an important reason why the item-based approach is still advantageous.

If an item that should have been marked as "Billable" when purchased, was in fact not marked appropriately, it will never get billed out to the customer and will never show up in a report on unbilled costs.

However, items are always used in Invoices or Sales Receipts. If an Expenses tab was inadvertently used in a purchase transaction, this will be caught by the Item Profitability report. Once the line item is fixed, the Item Profitability report will work as intended, and catch any items that were not passed through appropriately.

There's more...

One may argue that simply using one expense account for both purchase and sale transactions could also do the trick. If the account balance is zero, then there are no pass-through errors. However, in many cases, this account is also where non-pass-through expenses are classified, such as postage for the office versus reimbursable postage. If a non-zero balance indicates an error, it is a time-consuming process of narrowing the search to find the exact transaction. The Item Profitability report automatically eliminates entire batches of transactions and dramatically speeds up the work.

4

Special Tools

In this chapter, we will cover the following recipes:

- ▶ Using the History button
- ▶ Running the Transaction Journal report
- ▶ Producing a single-transaction audit trail
- ▶ Extracting customer and vendor histories
- ▶ Distinguishing between the Search and Find tools

Introduction

This chapter enables you to smoothly navigate through linked transactions, quickly view the **General Ledger** effect of a transaction, and efficiently locate transactions and other relevant information.

The following table is the **Recipe Reference Card** for the keyboard shortcuts included in this chapter:

History	Ctrl+H
Find	Ctrl+F
Transaction Journal	Ctrl+Y
Customize report	Alt+M
OK	Ctrl+Enter
Quick report	Ctrl+Q
All	A
Search	F3

Using the History button

With this recipe, you will be able to quickly navigate through the linked transactions, and produce a printable report showing the details of those linkages. Uses for this information include aligning the application of payments to the vendor and customer records, as well as confirming whether a transaction stamped as **PAID** was actually paid with cash, or if it was written off or discharged in some other manner.

Getting ready

Make sure that your accounting records include paid bills and invoices.

Display a bill or invoice which has been partially or fully paid and recorded.

How to do it...

1. On the upper bar above the data entry portion of the screen, below the **Icon** bar, click on the **History** button (*Ctrl+H*).
2. In the pop-up screen, view a list of linked transactions.
3. To navigate to one of the linked transactions, either double-click on it, or select it and click on the **Go To** button.
4. To prepare a report of all transactions linked to your bill or invoice, click on **Print**.
5. Either print the report or simply view it, by clicking on the **Preview** button.

There's more...

Certain types of transactions are automatically linked and can be navigated with the **History** button.

It's easy to remember linkages with the following patterns:

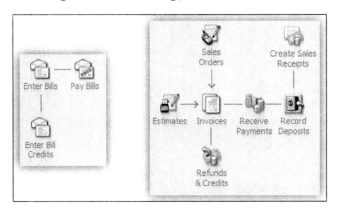

The one-way arrows indicate that once an invoice is created from an estimate or sales order, the **History** button can be used to navigate from the estimate or sales order to the invoice. To navigate in the opposite direction:

1. Open the invoice.

2. Make sure that the right-hand margin containing the customer (job) history is open:

3. Any sales orders or estimates used to create the invoice appear in the customer history:

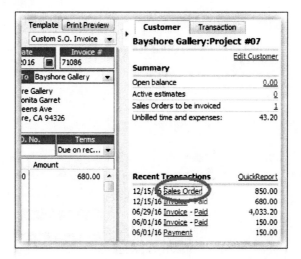

Alternatively, if you customize your invoice template to include a **S.O. No.** field, then you can use the link from the invoice to navigate to the **Sales Order**:

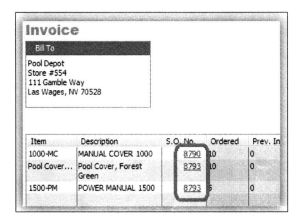

Furthermore, what causes transactions to be linked is a function of the General Ledger account in use, not the data entry screen. Therefore, if any journal entries include Accounts Receivable or Accounts Payable, and are applied to other transactions using the same accounts, then they will also be linked and navigable using the **History** button:

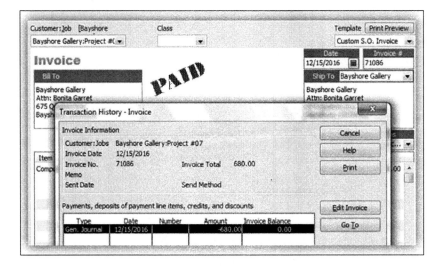

There are no links created between billable expenses and the invoices on which those expenses are billed.

Running the Transaction Journal report

Use this recipe to quickly identify the General Ledger effects of a transaction, whether or not a transaction has cleared, when the transaction was entered or last modified, and who entered or last modified a transaction.

Getting ready

Using the **Find** button (or **Edit | Find** or *Ctrl+F*) or other means, display a saved transaction. To get the strongest view of the clarity that the Transaction Journal brings, search for an item-based transaction, such as an invoice, sales receipt, or bill, in which the **Items** tab is used, or Payroll Liability Check.

How to do it...

1. Click the **Journal** button (*Ctrl+Y*).

2. Widen the columns as desired to view the **Account**, **Debit**, and **Credit** for the transaction.

3. Click on the **Customize Report** button (*Alt+M*).

4. On the **Display** tab, click on **Entered/Last Modified**, **Last modified by**, **Clr**, and/or other categories as desired, in the **Columns** box.

5. Click on the checked-off column headers that you wish to remove from the report.

6. Click on **OK** (*Ctrl+Enter*).

There's more...

Common uses for the Transaction Journal include:

Data entry screen	Use
Any item-based screen	Verify that the items affected the correct General Ledger accounts
Invoice, sales receipt	View the inventory valuation for a particular sale
Make deposits	See whether a particular deposit cleared without having to scroll through the ledger or register
Any transaction	See when it was entered or last modified, and by whom

If you call up a saved transaction using the **Find** feature, save a few steps by clicking on the **Find** screen's **Report** button, instead of opening up the transaction, and then opening up the Transaction Journal. This report shows the same information as the Transaction Journal, and can be customized in the same fashion.

Producing a single-transaction audit trail

With this recipe, you will be able to not only see when a single transaction was entered or last modified, as in the previous recipe, but also quickly see a report containing the complete change history for the transaction.

Getting ready

Open a bill, purchase order, invoice, sales receipt, or credit memo for a particular vendor or customer of interest.

How to do it...

1. Make sure the right-hand margin containing the customer (job or vendor) history is open:

2. This margin contains two tabs. The **Transaction** tab contains a record of the most recent changes.

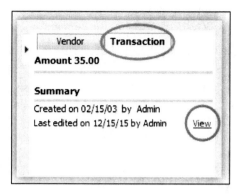

3. Click on the **View** link to view the full **Audit Trail** report for this transaction. Items in bold signify the changes made to a transaction.

There's more...

As always, you may use the **Customize Report** button to customize columns, add filters, and change other attributes of the report.

Extracting customer and vendor histories

The ultimate purposes of this recipe are to enable you to manage those aspects of customer relationships, which are based on transaction history, as well as to pull essential business intelligence from your accounting system, for use in management decision-making.

Getting ready

In order to benefit from these procedures, the customer and vendor names need to have been included with the transactions when recorded in QuickBooks:

Transaction type	Do	Don't
Credit card charges	Use the **Enter Credit Card Charges** screen for each individual charge	Batch-record the entire credit card bill in one screen
Accounts Payable	Enter individual bills for vendors	Batch-record expenses in one screen
Sales	Enter invoices, sales receipts, and/or deposits with the appropriate customer names	Enter batch deposits
Petty cash*	Set up a bank account to hold cash transactions	Periodically make a batch journal entry to expense cash items, or record cash customer deposits into the checking account

* This recommendation assumes that petty cash transactions, be they customer-related or vendor-related, are material.

How to do it...

View recent history:

1. Open a bill, purchase order, invoice, sales receipt, or credit memo for a particular vendor or customer of interest.

2. Make sure that the right-hand margin containing the customer (job or vendor) history is open:

3. This margin contains two tabs. The **Vendor** tab (or **Customer** tab, if you opened a customer-related transaction) displays the recent transaction history for that vendor (or customer):

QuickReport: Three instant ways to run the report:

1. From the previous screen, click on the **QuickReport** link, and set the date range as desired to run a broader report in terms of date range, and other characteristics available through the **Customize Report** button.

2. From any data entry screen with a name already selected, press *Ctrl+Q*.

3. From the **Vendors** tab in the **Vendor Center**, or from the **Customers & Jobs** tab in the **Customer Center**, or from another list, select the desired name, and press *Ctrl+Q*.

The default date range for a **QuickReport** produced by *Ctrl+Q* is **This Month-to-date**. To quickly broaden the date range to **All**, immediately after opening the report press the letter *A* on your keyboard.

Distinguishing between the the Search and Find tools

Use this recipe to quickly retrieve specific information from your QuickBooks file. This information can be as diverse as transactions, vendor contact information, item descriptions, and much more.

Getting ready

If desired, make sure the **Search Box** is in the **Icon** bar. If not, click on **View | Search Box**.

How to do it...

1. Type a word, phrase, or dollar amount in the **Search Box** (*F3*). Click on the **Search** icon to the right of the box, or press your *Enter* key.

2. In the list of results, either mouse over and click on a transaction, or other result displayed, or narrow results, by using one of the on-screen filters:

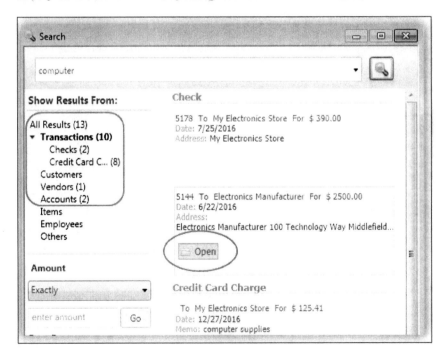

3. Apply a filter, for example the **Accounts** filter, to view only the search results pertaining to **Accounts**:

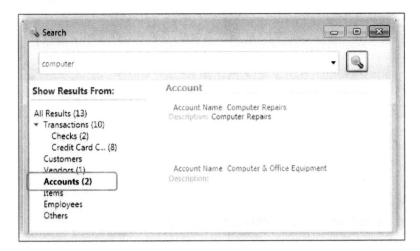

There's more...

Unlike the **Find** feature, the **Search** feature displays not only transactions, but any field from any data entry field in QuickBooks, be it customer information, a default inventory price, or a memo. Use **Find** and **Search** strategically, depending on whether you want a narrow set of results based on a criteria for a certain field, or if you prefer a broader range of results across multiple fields.

 The **Find** feature includes a **Report** button to prepare a printable report with customizable columns. The **Search** feature includes no such report.

5
Customizing Reports

In this chapter, we will cover:

- ▶ Creating an "Unearned income by customer" report
- ▶ Creating an "Accrued interest payable by lender" report
- ▶ Creating an "Uncleared transactions" report
- ▶ Capturing unbilled items simultaneously
- ▶ Memorizing reports
- ▶ Sharing reports
- ▶ Preparing a custom Profit & Loss report with the QuickBooks Statement Writer

Introduction

By the end of this chapter, you will be able to create meaningful reports beyond those which are readily available in the **QuickBooks Report Center**. You will also be adept at preserving and organizing highly customized reports.

The following table is the **Recipe Reference Card** for the keyboard shortcuts included in this chapter:

Copy	Ctrl+C
Paste	Ctrl+V
Chart of Accounts	Ctrl+A
Memorize a report	Ctrl+M

Creating an "Unearned income by customer" report

Use this recipe to track the balances of your upfront deposits on a customer-by-customer or job-by-job basis. The same technique can be applied to other balance sheet accounts.

Getting ready

For this procedure to be effective, all transactions involving the Unearned Income account, be they customer deposits, retainers, refunds, invoices, or revenue recognition journal entries, should be entered into the **QuickBooks file**, with the Customer:Job or Name field filled out consistently.

How to do it...

1. Select **Reports | Custom Reports | Summary**.
2. On the **Display** tab, set the **Dates** and **Display rows by** fields as shown in the following screenshot:

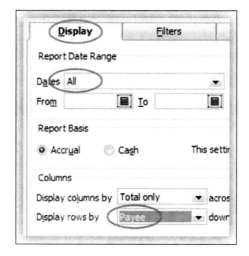

3. If you wish to set a cut-off date, enter a date in the **To** field, but leave the **From** field blank, in order to show cumulative balances correctly. On the same tab, click on the **Advanced Options** button, and select **Display Rows | Non-zero**, as shown in the following screenshot:

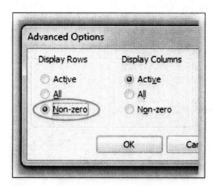

4. If you choose a variation of this report, and break out columns by some other criteria such as Time Period or Customer Type, consider also selecting **Non-zero** in the **Display Columns** portion of the **Advanced** box, as shown in the preceding screenshot.

5. On the **Filters** tab, in the **Choose Filter** box, click on **Select Account**.

6. From the drop-down box, select **Unearned Income** or the name of the comparable account in your Chart of Accounts.

7. Highlight the name of the account and copy it (right-click | **Copy** or *Ctrl+C*).

8. On the **Header/Footer** tab, in the **Report Title** field, paste the account name (right-click | **Paste** or *Ctrl+V*), and type **by Customer**, as shown in the following screenshot:

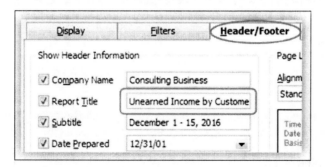

9.   Click on **OK** to reveal your customized report, as shown in the following screenshot:

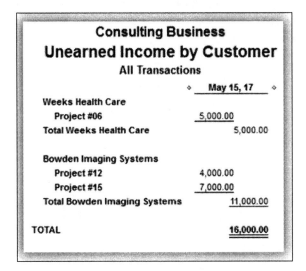

 If you track customer activity by job, use the **Collapse/Expand** button to see the preceding report on a customer-by-customer basis, or a job-by-job basis. If you prefer an expanded report, consider renaming the report as "Unearned Income by Project" or "Unearned Income by Job".

Creating an "Accrued interest payable by lender" report

For companies with multiple creditors, this recipe is valuable in tracking the balances of your accrued interest liabilities on a lender-by-lender basis. One advantage of this approach is the opportunity to maintain a simple Chart of Accounts, instead of a complex one including subaccounts for each lender. The same technique can be applied to other balance sheet accounts.

Although the technique is similar to the previous recipe, this example includes an additional level of complexity, namely the use of both current and long-term liability accounts.

Getting ready

For this procedure to be effective, all interest accruals and payments, be they journal entries, checks, bills, or other related transactions, should be entered into the QuickBooks file with the **Payee** or **Vendor** or **Name** field filled out consistently.

How to do it...

1. Select **Reports | Custom Reports | Summary**.

2. On the **Display** tab, arrange the **Date**, **Display columns by**, and **Display rows by** fields, as shown in the following screenshot:

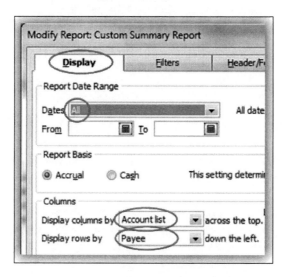

3. If you wish to set a cut-off date, enter a date in the **To** field, but leave the **From** field blank, in order to show cumulative balances correctly. On the same tab, click on the **Advanced Options** button, and select **Display Rows | Non-zero** and **Display Columns | Non-zero**, as shown in the following screenshot:

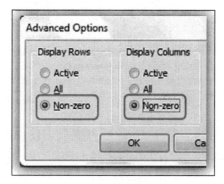

4. On the **Filters** tab, in the **Choose Filter** box, click on **Select Account**.

5. In the drop-down box, scroll to the top of the list, and select **Multiple accounts**.

6. In the pop-up box, click to select your current and long-term accrued interest payable accounts, as marked in red in the following screenshot:

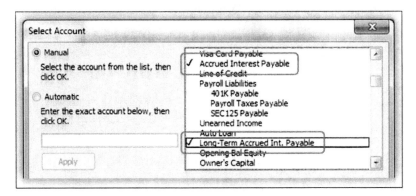

7. On the **Header/Footer** tab, in the **Report Title** field, enter the title **Accrued Interest by Lender**, as shown in the following screenshot:

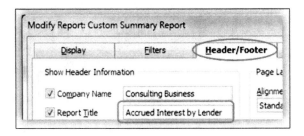

8. Click on **OK** to reveal your customized report as follows:

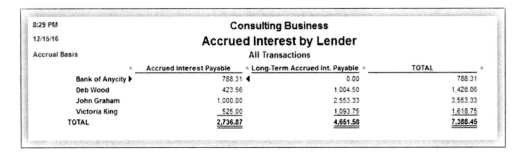

8:29 PM 12/15/16 Accrual Basis	Accrued Interest Payable	Long-Term Accrued Int. Payable	TOTAL
Bank of Anycity	788.31	0.00	788.31
Deb Wood	423.56	1,004.50	1,428.06
John Graham	1,000.00	2,553.33	3,553.33
Victoria King	525.00	1,093.75	1,618.75
TOTAL	2,736.87	4,651.58	7,388.45

If you accrue all interest as current and then periodically reclassify certain balances as long term (or vice-versa), make sure that the reclassifying journal entry includes lender name on a separate line for both the current and long-term accounts.

Creating an "Uncleared transactions" report

The bank reconciliation report shows a great deal of information beyond a simple list of uncleared transactions. Use this recipe to prepare a straightforward list of uncleared transactions, whether or not the account is reconciled. Practical applications include the Undeposited Funds account, which does not get reconciled but does include the cleared status of funds.

How to do it...

1. Prepare a ledger report for the desired account. A straightforward way to do this is to select **Reports | Company & Financial | Balance Sheet Standard**, and then double-click on the desired account. Running a quick report from the Chart of Accounts (*Ctrl+A*) is also an alternative, although the **Clr** field is not displayed by default in that report.

2. Click on the **Customize Report** button.

3. On the **Filters** tab, in the **Choose Filter** box, scroll down, and select **Cleared | No**.

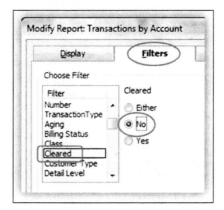

4. On the **Header/Footer** tab, in the **Report Title** field, enter **Uncleared Transactions**, as shown in the following screenshot:

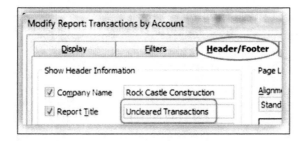

5. Click on **OK** to reveal your customized report. Remove unneeded columns if necessary; the result is shown in the following screenshot:

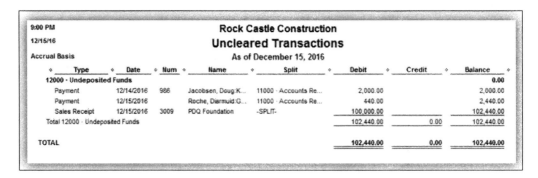

There's more...

Variations of this report include:

▸ Showing all bank accounts by adding an **Account** filter in the **Filters** tab, and selecting **All bank accounts**

▸ Showing selected accounts by adding an **Account** filter in the **Filters** tab, selecting **Multiple account**, and checking off each desired account

▸ Showing only the uncleared checks by adding a **Transaction Type** filter in the **Filters** tab, selecting either **Checks** or **Multiple Transaction Types | Checks | Bill Payment | Sales Tax Payment**

▸ Showing only the cleared items by clicking on **Yes** instead of **No** in the **Cleared** filter

Capturing unbilled items simultaneously

If you bill time, expenses, or mileage, to your customers, this recipe will be instrumental in capturing all of those unbilled items at once. It is then up to you to ensure that these items are billed to your customer!

Getting ready

Make sure you have recorded billable time, expenses, and/or mileage, for your customers. A comprehensive effort is not necessary to see how this recipe works, but is recommended for these reports to garner greatest customer reimbursement.

How to do it...

1. Set up a memorized report group, as follows:

   ❑ Select **Reports | Memorized Reports | Memorized Report List**

   ❑ From the bottom-left corner of the screen, click on the **Memorized Report** button, followed by **New Group**

   ❑ Name the group **Unbilled Items** and click on **OK**

2. Memorize a report of unbilled time as follows:

   ❑ Select **Reports | Jobs, Time & Mileage | Time by Job Detail**

   ❑ Click on the **Customize Report** button, and from the **Filters** tab, add the **Billing Status** filter of **Unbilled**, as shown in the following screenshot:

   ❑ On the **Header/Footer** tab, rewrite the **Report Title** to read **Unbilled Time by Job**, or another title meaningful to you, as shown in the following screenshot:

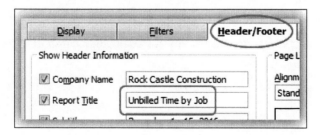

- From the **Display** tab, or after clicking on **OK** to return to the report, use the **Dates** drop-down box to change the **Date Range** to **All**. The completed report resembles the following screenshot:

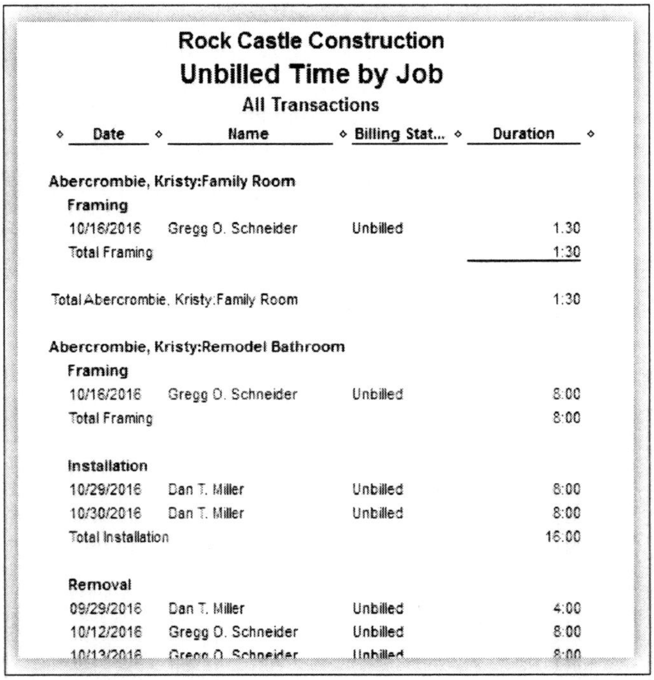

Rock Castle Construction
Unbilled Time by Job
All Transactions

Date	Name	Billing Stat...	Duration
Abercrombie, Kristy:Family Room			
Framing			
10/16/2016	Gregg O. Schneider	Unbilled	1:30
Total Framing			1:30
Total Abercrombie, Kristy:Family Room			1:30
Abercrombie, Kristy:Remodel Bathroom			
Framing			
10/16/2016	Gregg O. Schneider	Unbilled	8:00
Total Framing			8:00
Installation			
10/29/2016	Dan T. Miller	Unbilled	8:00
10/30/2016	Dan T. Miller	Unbilled	8:00
Total Installation			16:00
Removal			
09/29/2016	Dan T. Miller	Unbilled	4:00
10/12/2016	Gregg O. Schneider	Unbilled	8:00
10/13/2016	Gregg O. Schneider	Unbilled	8:00

- Click on the **Memorize** button (*Ctrl+M*)
- The report name appears automatically in the Name field. Check off the **Memorized Report Group** box, and select **Unbilled Items**, the report group that you created in the previous portion of this recipe, from the drop-down box.

3. Memorize a report of unbilled costs, as follows:
   - Select **Reports** | **Customers & Receivables** | **Unbilled Costs by Job**
   - Arrange the columns as needed
   - Use the **Dates** drop-down box to change the **Date Range** to **All**; the completed report resembles the following screenshot:

Rock Castle Construction
Unbilled Costs by Job
All Transactions

Type	Date	Source Name	Billing Status	Amount
Abercrombie, Kristy				
Kitchen				
Check	12/15/2016	Vu Contracting	Unbilled	1,000.00
Total Kitchen				1,000.00
Total Abercrombie, Kristy				1,000.00
Rahn, Jennifer				
Remodel				
Bill	06/07/2016	Zeng Building Supplies	Unbilled	0.00
Bill	06/07/2016	Zeng Building Supplies	Unbilled	11,807.80
Bill	06/07/2016	Zeng Building Supplies	Unbilled	-4,368.51
Bill	06/07/2016	Zeng Building Supplies	Unbilled	4,368.51
Total Remodel				11,807.80
Total Rahn, Jennifer				11,807.80
Yoo, Young-Kyu				
Repairs				
Bill	01/02/2016	A Cheung Limited	Unbilled	1,500.00
Total Repairs				1,500.00
Total Yoo, Young-Kyu				1,500.00

❑ Click on the **Memorize** button (*Ctrl+M*)

❑ The report name appears automatically in the Name field. Check off the **Memorized Report Group** box and select **Unbilled Items**, the report group that you created in the previous portion of this recipe, from the drop-down box.

4. Memorize a report of unassigned costs, as follows:

❑ **Contractor Edition**: Select **Reports | Contractor Reports | Expenses Not Assigned to Jobs**

❑ **Professional Services Edition**: Select **Reports | Professional Services Reports | Expenses Not Assigned to Projects**

❑ **Accountant Edition**: Select **Reports | Industry Specific | Contractor Reports | Expenses Not Assigned to Jobs**, or **Reports | Industry Specific | Professional Services Reports | Expenses Not Assigned to Projects**

❑ The purpose of this report is to capture billable costs not assigned to a customer accidentally, and therefore absent from any of the other reports in this recipe. If there are certain classes or expense accounts that exclusively include expenses that are not billable or assignable to customers, click on the **Customize** button and use the **Filters** to only include certain accounts or classes.

❑ Use the **Dates** drop-down box to change the **Date Range** to **All**; the completed report resembles the following screenshot:

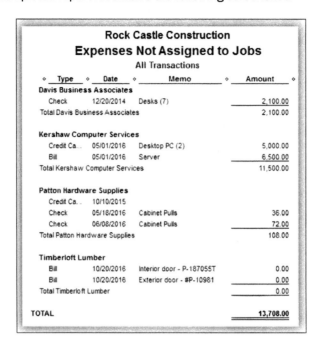

❑ Click on the **Memorize** button (*Ctrl+M*)

❑ The report name appears automatically in the **Name** field. Check off the **Memorized Report Group** box and select **Unbilled Items**, the report group that you created in the previous portion of this recipe, from the drop-down box.

5. Memorize a report of unbilled mileage, as follows:

❑ Select **Reports | Jobs, Time, & Mileage | Mileage by Job Detail**.

❑ Click on the **Customize Report** button, and from the **Filters** tab, add the **Billing Status** filter of **Unbilled**, as shown in the following screenshot:

❑ From the **Header/Footer** tab, rewrite the **Report Title** to read **Unbilled Mileage by Job**, or another title meaningful to you, as shown in the following screenshot:

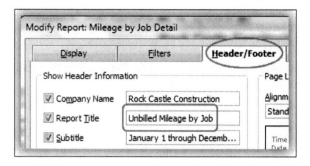

❑ From the **Display** tab, or after clicking on **OK** to return to the report, use the **Dates** drop-down box to change the **Date Range** to **All**.

❑ Adjust columns as desired. The completed report resembles the following screenshot:

Rock Castle Construction
Unbilled Mileage by Job
All Transactions

Vehicle	Trip End Date	Billing Stat...	Total Miles	Sales Price	Amount
Abercrombie, Kristy					
Family Room					
2002 Ford Truck	06/15/2016	Billable	18	0.365	6.57
2001 Chevy Minivan	06/16/2016	Billable	92	0.365	33.58
1998 Saturn	06/17/2016	Billable	51	0.365	18.62
1998 Saturn	06/19/2016	Billable	15	0.365	5.48
1998 Saturn	06/19/2016	Billable	16	0.365	5.84
2002 Ford Truck	06/22/2016	Billable	71	0.365	25.92
2001 Chevy Minivan	08/06/2016	Billable	11	0.365	4.02
1998 Saturn	08/13/2016	Billable	49	0.365	17.89
2002 Ford Truck	09/23/2016	Billable	48	0.365	17.52
Total Family Room			371		135.44
Total Abercrombie, Kristy			371		135.44
Barley, Renee					
2002 Ford Truck	06/17/2016	Billable	35	0.365	12.78
1998 Saturn	06/18/2016	Billable	32	0.365	11.68
2001 Chevy Minivan	06/19/2016	Billable	63	0.365	23.00
2002 Ford Truck	07/02/2016	Billable	44	0.365	16.06

❑ Click on the **Memorize** button (*Ctrl+M*)

❑ The report name appears automatically in the **Name** field. Check off the **Memorized Report Group** box and select **Unbilled Items**, the report group that you created in the previous portion of this recipe, from the drop-down box.

6. Run all unbilled item reports simultaneously, as follows:

   ❑ Select **Reports | Memorized Reports | Memorized Report List**

   ❑ Double-click on the heading of **Unbilled Items**

7. An alternative to the preceding steps are as follows:

   ❑ Select **Reports | Process Multiple Reports**

   ❑ Select **Unbilled Items** from the drop-down box, and then continue as shown in the following screenshot:

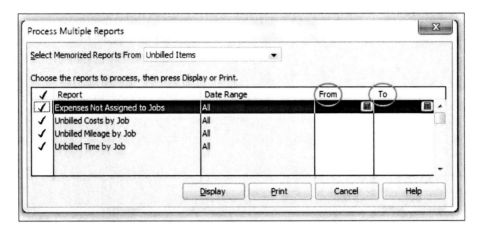

8. If you desire a **Date Range** other than **All**, enter it in the **From** and **To** fields.

9. Click on **Display** or **Print**.

Memorizing reports

Use this recipe to save time by storing your most important and highly customized reports, while having convenient access to these reports. This recipe is also relevant in updating the parameters of previously memorized reports.

How to do it...

1. Create a memorized report, as follows:

   ❑ Using conventional means, create a report of your choice.

   ❑ If applicable, customize the report as desired.

   ❑ Click on the **Memorize** button (*Ctrl+M*).

□ The report name appears automatically in the **Name** field. If you wish to add the report to a group, check off the **Memorized Report Group** box, and select a **Report Group** from the drop-down box.

2. Run Memorized Report, as follows:

□ Select **Reports | Memorized Reports | Memorized Report List**.

□ Double-click on the report of your choice.

□ If you wish to simultaneously run several reports in a group, double-click on the group name instead.

3. Update Memorized Report, as follows:

□ Using the preceding steps, run Memorized Report.

□ Change the parameters of the report.

□ Click on the **Memorize** button (*Ctrl+M*).

□ When prompted, click on **Replace**, as shown in the following screenshot:

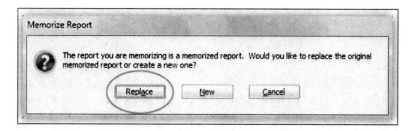

□ If you have customized your report to such an extent that it now appears a different report to you, click on **New** instead, and fill out the **Memorize Report** screen, as shown in the following screenshot:

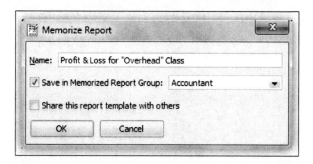

There's more...

If you frequently access the list of memorized reports, add the **Memorized Report List** to your icon bar, as follows:

1. Select **Reports | Memorized Reports | Memorized Report List**.

2. Select **View | Add Window to Icon Bar**.

3. If desired, change **Icon**, **Label**, or **Description**. Click on **OK**, as shown in the following screenshot:

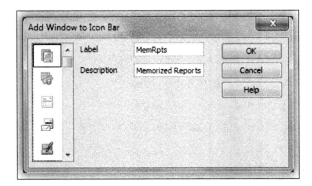

 If you frequently need to change the parameters of memorized reports, it is more efficient to save that report as a memorized report than to add the report to your icon bar. Memorized reports can be updated using the preceding recipe to replace the previous report, while reports added to the icon bar must be removed, updated, and added again to the icon bar.

Sharing reports

Follow this recipe to contribute your customized report to the community of QuickBooks users.

Getting ready

Make sure your Internet connection is active.

How to do it...

1. Run a report, and customize it as desired.

2. On the report, click on the **Share Template** button, as shown in the following screenshot:

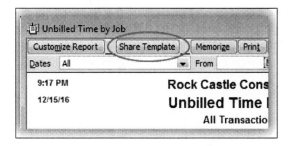

3. In the pop-up window, there are two tabs. In the first tab, named **Basic Info**, the **Report Title** appears automatically. Leave this, or overwrite it if you wish.

4. Fill the **Description** field, which describes not just what the report contains, but also the benefit of using the report as shown in the following screenshot. This is the language that will cause a fellow QuickBooks user to download your report:

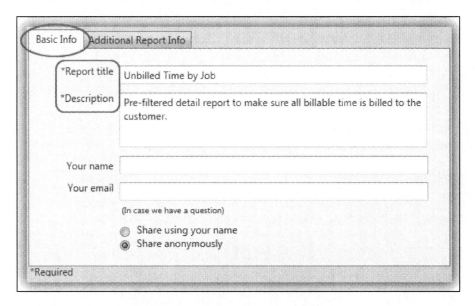

5. Other fields are not required. Fill them in at your discretion.

6. Click on the **Additional Report Info** tab. In the **Report Type** drop-down box, you will see familiar report categories. Select the appropriate category for your report, as shown in the following screenshot:

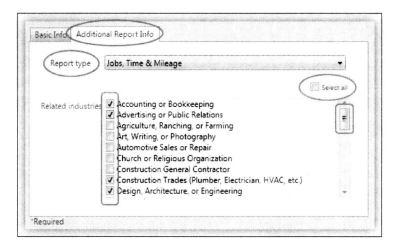

7. An optional field is **Related industries**. Use the checkboxes, if desired, to help other QuickBooks users find your report. Use the **Select all** checkbox and the scroll bar to assist you in this process.

8. On completion, click on the **Shared** button. After a moment, you will see a pop-up message notifying you that your report has been shared.

There's more...

At this point, three things occur in your QuickBooks file. They are as follows:

1. Your report is now included in the **Report Center**, in the **Memorized** tab, beneath the **Shared** section, as shown in the following screenshot:

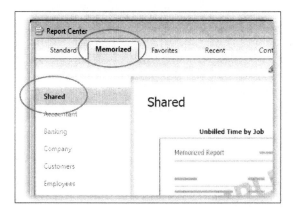

2. A related change is that QuickBooks automatically adds a **Shared** group, containing your report in your **Memorized Report List**, as shown in the following screenshot:

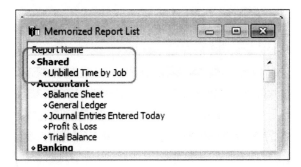

3. Additionally, your report is now visible to the community as a contributed report.

You need to perform the following steps to access your Report Center:

1. Select **Reports | Report Center**, or click on the **Report Center** button if it is on your icon bar, as shown in the following screenshot:

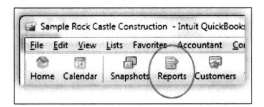

2. Click on the **Contributed Reports** tab.

3. From the **View industry** drop-down box, select one of the industries that you checked off while you shared your report.

4. In the left-hand margin, click on the report category that you selected while you shared your report.

5. If many reports appear, select **Community created** in the **Sort by** drop-down box.

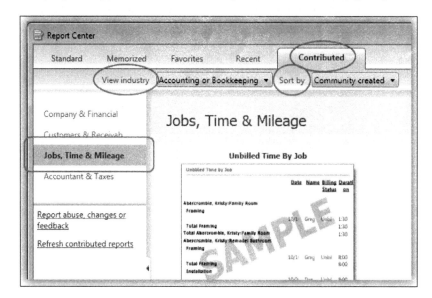

Make sure you have downloaded all the latest updates for QuickBooks, so that the contributed reports list refreshes properly when your shared report does not appear in the list.

In the **Contributed** tab, use the **Sort by** drop-down box to select **Community created**. Then, you will see a refreshed link of contributed reports on the left-hand margin. If your report is not in the list, click on this link, or press *Ctrl* and click on it to force a refresh of the page.

Preparing a custom Profit & Loss report with the QuickBooks Statement Writer

Use this recipe to create customized reports with **QuickBooks Statement Writer** (**QSW**). The main advantage of QSW is the ability to present information in the form of account balances in a desired format, while allowing for information updates. Although the software wizard does allow for certain customizations, knowledge of Excel techniques is the key for expert workarounds to produce the reports that you need.

To illustrate the power of QSW, this recipe focuses on including selected Balance Sheet information in a Profit & Loss report. Please note that this recipe, as a part of the book for experts, does not include a step-by-step procedure on how to set up a basic, uncustomized report in the QSW.

Getting ready

1. To access the QSW, select **Reports | QuickBooks Statement Writer | Design New**.

2. Use the QSW to prepare a single-period **Income Statement** and **Cash Flow** statement, as shown in the following screenshot:

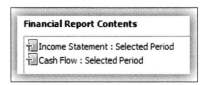

3. No additional customizations are needed for this recipe. So, proceed through the wizard by clicking on the **Next** button a number of times, and finally clicking on the **Create Report** button. Microsoft Excel will open, and your reports will be displayed as shown in the following screenshot:

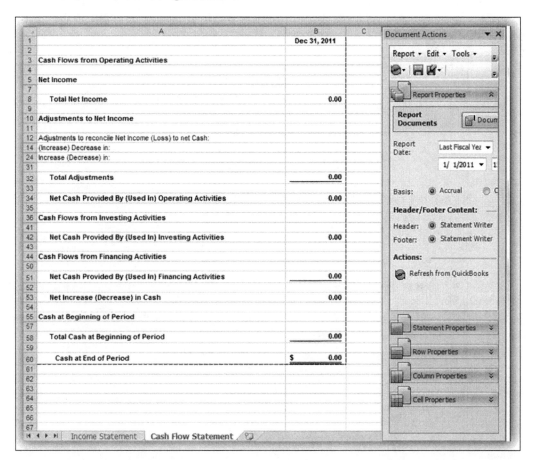

How to do it...

1. Click on the **Income Statement** tab and scroll to the bottom of the report, as shown in the following screenshot:

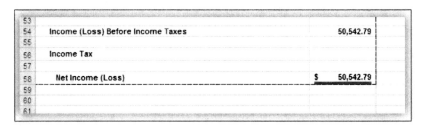

2. Following the **Net Income (Loss)** line, type **Selected Account Information** and format as desired.

3. Move the cursor to the next row. Type **=**, and click on the **Cash Flow Statement** tab.

4. Click on the cell containing the words **(Increase) Decrease in**, as shown in the following screenshot:

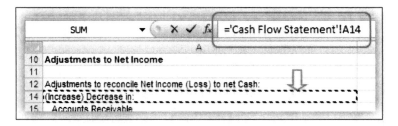

5. Hit the *Enter* key and view the result on the **Profit & Loss** tab, as shown in the following screenshot:

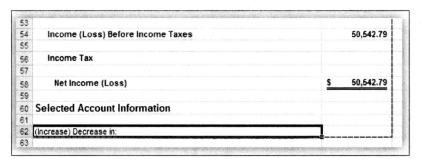

6. Using the same method, or by copying and pasting the links, bring the desired accounts and their balance changes to the income statement by linking them from the **Cash Flow Statement** tab, to generate the report shown in the following screenshot:

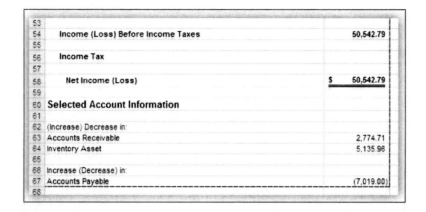

7. Hide the **Cash Flow Statement** tab, if it is of no interest to your report users, by right-clicking on the tab and selecting **Hide**, as shown in the following screenshot:

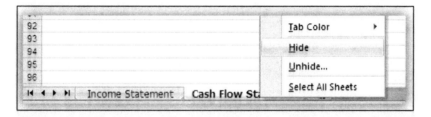

8. Change the report header as needed, to reflect the additional information. If your report header is an Excel header instead of spreadsheet cells, access the report header in one of the following ways:

   ❑ Select **Insert | Header & Footer** (Excel 2007 and 2010)

   ❑ Select **View | Page Layout** (Excel 2007 and 2010)

   ❑ Select **Page Layout | Page Setup group | Page Setup** pop-up box | **Header/Footer** tab | **Custom Header** (Excel 2007 and 2010)

   ❑ Select **File | Page Setup | Header/Footer** tab | **Custom Header** (Excel 2003)

   ❑ Select **View | Header & Footer** (Excel 2003)

6
Memorized Transactions

In this chapter, we will cover the following recipes:

- ▸ Memorizing transactions for automatic entry
- ▸ Memorizing transactions for assisted entry
- ▸ Editing a memorized transaction
- ▸ Configuring reminders for memorized transactions
- ▸ Grouping memorized transactions

Introduction

In this chapter, you will be able to use the techniques to eliminate and reduce the data entry time, and increase the accuracy of repetitive transactions. You will also be able to keep these shortcuts organized and accessible.

The following table is the **Recipe Reference Card** for the keyboard shortcuts included in this chapter:

Memorize a transaction	Ctrl+M
Enter a memorized transaction	Alt+T
Memorized Transactions List	Ctrl+T
Close the screen	Esc
Delete item in list	Ctrl+D

Memorizing transactions for automatic entry

When your business executes repetitive and periodic transactions in which every field in use is constant, then automated entry saves a great deal of time and effort. Use this recipe to program QuickBooks to perform data entry for you!

Getting ready

Display or create a transaction that is frequently repeated, completely filled with all of the information that you wish to include in the **template**, which is the memorized transaction. Use the following guide to determine whether the transaction that you have in mind can be memorized by QuickBooks:

Can be memorized	Cannot be memorized
Invoice	Time/single activity
Credit memo	Paycheck
Sales receipt	Inventory adjustment
Statement charge	Sales tax payment
Estimate	Bill payment
Sales order	Customer payment
Purchase order	Build assembly
Bill	
Credit	
Credit card charge	
Credit card credit	
Check	
Deposit	
Payroll liability check	
Journal entry	

How to do it...

1. From the **Edit** menu, select **Memorize** (*Ctrl+M*).
2. In the **Name** field, enter a descriptive and easy-to-remember title for your memorized transaction.

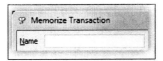

The **Name** field does not appear on the face of the transaction itself, but shows how you can find your transaction in the **Memorized Transactions** list.

3. Select **Automate Transaction Entry**, so that QuickBooks enters this transaction automatically on the right date, with no further data entry required.

4. Complete the **How Often** field to establish the overall frequency of the transaction.

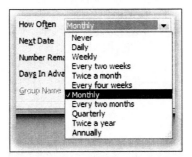

5. Complete the **Next Date** field to establish a pattern of dates for QuickBooks to follow:

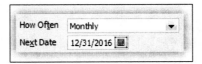

6. If in a previous step, you selected **Twice a month**, then fill in the **Subsequent Date** field in order to establish the date pattern for QuickBooks to follow:

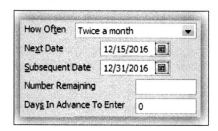

7. The **Number Remaining** field is optional, but can be useful in recording the transactions that are part of a finite series of transactions, such as bills for lease-to-own equipment, journal entries to expense prepaid insurance, or rent invoices for tenants for the remainder of the lease period.

8. The **Days In Advance To Enter** field is optional, and is most useful in the following situations:

Transaction type	Enter in Advance to...
Check	Add the check to the print queue in advance of sending the properly dated check
Invoice	Print or e-mail invoices in advance of the due date, but record the invoices as of a certain date
Bill	Add the bill to the **Unpaid Bills** list as a reminder to pay the bill, but retain the appropriate bill date

How it works...

The next time that the QuickBooks file is opened on or after the **Next Date** is entered in a previous step, the following screen will appear automatically, to alert you to execute the memorized transactions. In the following example, "today" is December 15, 2016:

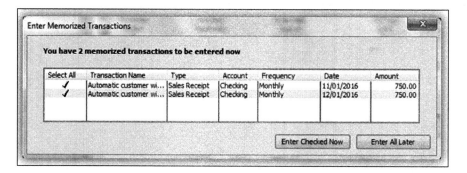

Either click on **Enter Checked Now** or deselect any individual transactions that you do not wish to be entered at this time.

Otherwise, click on **Enter All Later**.

Regardless of your choice, you will proceed to the normal QuickBooks operations.

 If you suddenly discover that you need to enter repetitive transactions to get caught up in some aspect of your accounting records, such as expensing prepaid insurance, then create it once as a back-dated automatic memorized transaction. Close and reopen the file, and you'll see the prompt to enter all eight months of journal entries, all at once!

Memorizing transactions for assisted entry

When your business executes repetitive, periodic transactions, in which most fields in use are constant, but at least one field changes from transaction to transaction, then the semi-automated entry is a template approach that saves a great deal of time and effort.

Getting ready

Display or create a transaction that is frequently repeated, completely filled with all of the information that you wish to include in the "template", which is the memorized transaction. For any fields that tend to change from transaction to transaction, such as the dollar amount, leave those fields blank.

Use the previous guide to determine whether the transaction that you have in mind can be memorized by QuickBooks.

How to do it...

1. From the **Edit** menu, select **Memorize** (*Ctrl+M*).

2. In the **Name** field, enter a descriptive, easy-to-remember title for your memorized transaction.

The **Name** field does not appear on the face of the transaction itself, but shows how you can find your transaction in the **Memorized Transactions** list.

3. Select **Add to my Reminders List,** regardless of whether you use that feature. More about the **Reminders List** is included later in this chapter.

4. Complete the **How Often** field to establish the overall frequency of the transactions.

5. Complete the **Next Date** field to establish a pattern of dates for QuickBooks to follow:

6. If in a previous step you selected **Twice a month**, then fill in the **Subsequent Date** field in order to establish the date pattern for QuickBooks to follow:

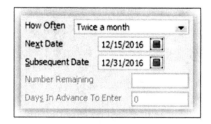

There's more...

If you use the Reminders list

Anytime you open the **Reminders** list, be it automatically when you open your QuickBooks file or at any other time, the **Memorized Transactions Due** section appears when at least one memorized transaction's entry date has occurred.

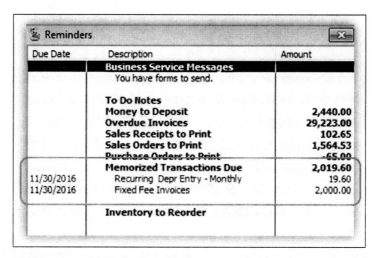

Double-click on the transaction of interest in the **Reminders** list, and QuickBooks will open the **Memorized Transaction List** and highlight the appropriate transaction.

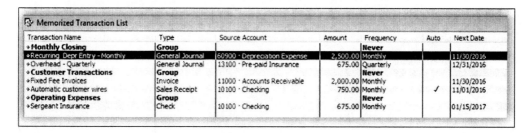

Double-click on the transaction (*Alt+T*) to begin the data entry process, adding any missing information, such as the dollar amount or memo, which is not already included in your "template".

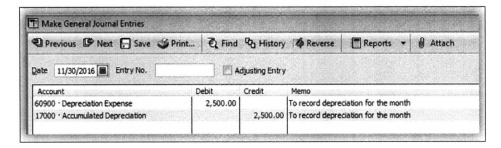

If you do not use the Reminders list

Periodically consult the **Memorized Transaction List** (**Lists | Memorized Transaction List** or *Ctrl+T*) to see whether any transactions need to be entered. Double-click on a transaction, or select it and press *Alt+T* to begin the data entry process, adding any missing information, such as the dollar amount or memo, which is not already included in your "template".

You may find it helpful to order your **Memorized Transaction List** by date. To do this, click on the **Next Date** heading in the list.

Editing a memorized transaction

After creating a memorized transaction, you can use this recipe to update the data entry fields within a memorized transaction for use in future transactions. This recipe also includes steps for editing the terms of the timing, or other attributes of the transaction.

Getting ready

Create at least one memorized transaction, and open the **Memorized Transaction List** (**Lists | Memorized Transaction List** or *Ctrl+T*).

How to do it...

To update the data entry fields within a memorized transaction, follow these steps:

1. Double-click on the memorized transaction, or select it and press *Alt+T*.
2. Modify the fields as desired.
3. From the **Edit** menu, select **Memorize** (*Ctrl+M*).
4. In the following prompt, click on **Replace**:

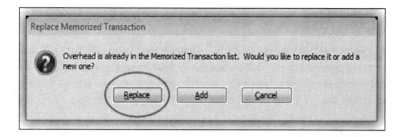

5. Close the screen without saving the transaction (*Esc*). In the following prompt, click on **No**:

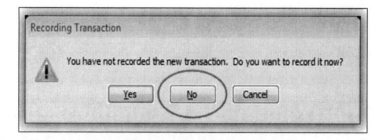

To edit the terms of the timing or other attributes of the transaction, follow these steps:

1. From the **Lists** menu, select **Memorized Transactions** (*Ctrl+T*).
2. Select the transaction.
3. From the **Edit** menu, select **Edit Memorized Transactions** (*Ctrl+E*).
4. Modify the terms as desired. Any of the fields in the following screenshot can be edited, and will not affect transactions already entered:

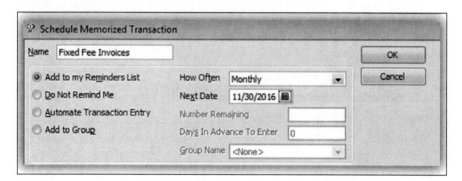

How it works...

When you distinguish the transaction from its memorization, you see that you can edit the fields or the terms of a transaction independently of any previously completed data entry. Be careful not to accidentally enter a transaction when you only mean to edit its terms or details, but, of course, accidentally entered transactions can always be deleted.

There's more...

To delete a memorized transaction from the list:

1. Select the transaction in the list.

2. From the **Edit** menu, select **Delete Memorized Transactions** (*Ctrl+D*).

Deleting a memorized transaction from the list does not impact any transactions already recorded.

Configuring reminders for memorized transactions

This recipe coordinates the **Reminders List** feature and the **Memorized Transactions** feature of QuickBooks. Set your reminders which work most effectively for your organization and your working style.

How to do it...

1. From the **Company** menu, select **Reminders**, followed by the **Set Preferences** button

   OR

   From the **Edit** menu, select **Preferences**, followed by **Reminders** in the left-hand margin.

2. Click on the **Company Preferences** tab.

3. In the **Memorized Transactions Due** row, select the summary or list view.

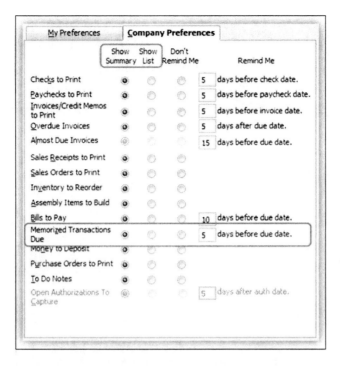

The **Show Summary** option causes only the **Memorized Transactions Due** heading to appear in the **Reminders** list, by default.

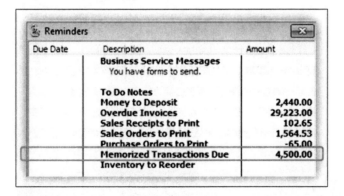

4. Double-click on the heading to show the list of the memorized transactions that are currently due.

5. Alternatively, the **Show List** selection in the **Preferences** window results in a **Reminders** list with all of the transactions listed.

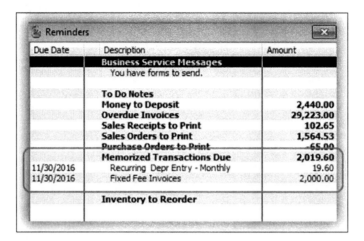

There's more...

In the **Preferences** window, in the **Reminders** section, click on the **My Preferences** tab to take advantage of the opportunity to see the **Reminders** list automatically, every time you open the QuickBooks file:

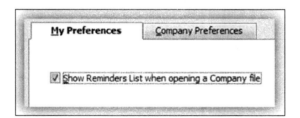

An alternative is to add the **Reminders** button to your icon bar; see *Chapter 2, Customizing the Interface*, for the *Customizing the icon bar* recipe.

Grouping memorized transactions

Use this recipe to execute multiple transactions on the same time schedule. A bonus recipe includes a clever way to use memorized transaction groups, to visually organize the **Memorized Transaction List**.

Getting ready

Create at least two memorized transactions, and open the **Memorized Transaction List** (**Lists | Memorized Transaction List** or *Ctrl+T*).

How to do it...

Execute multiple transactions simultaneously:

1. To create a memorized transaction group, click on the **Memorized Transaction** button, and select **New Group** from the submenu.

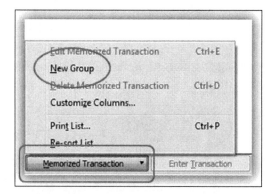

2. Enter the terms for the group, as described in the previous recipes in this chapter.

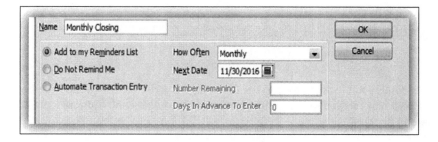

3. Once a group is created, click and hold each diamond to drag the existing memorized transactions below the group name as illustrated in the following screenshot:

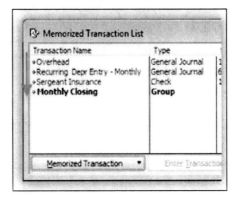

4. Then, drag the diamonds to the right, to be indented below the group heading.

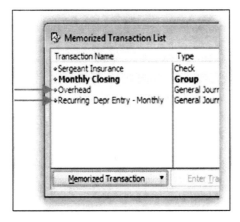

5. The final result looks similar to the following screenshot, and group members should now be able to share the transaction frequency and automation as the group heading:

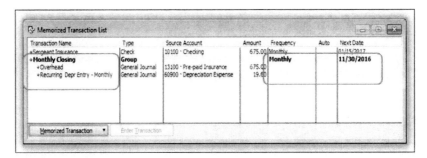

6. As an alternative to the preceding steps, edit existing memorized transactions or create new memorized transactions, and select **Add to Group** and enter a **Group Name**:

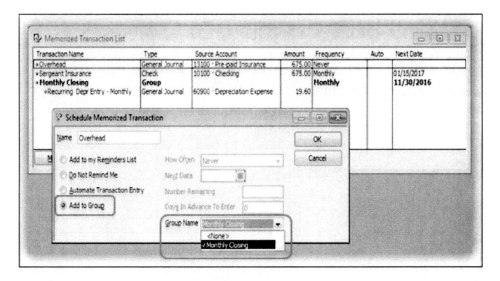

Use **Groups** to visually organize the **Memorized Transaction List**:

1. Create the **New Group** as indicated in the previous screenshot, and select **Do Not Remind Me** for the transaction scheduling.

2. By left-clicking the diamond, and holding down the mouse button, drag the other memorized transactions below this group name:

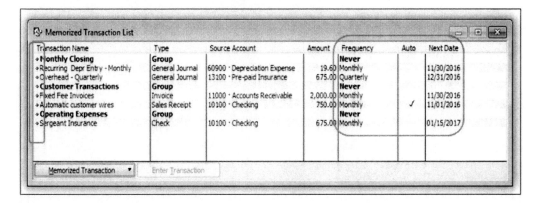

How it works...

Grouped transactions share scheduling and automation, but the information contained within each transaction in the group is distinct and independent.

There's more...

For grouped transactions that are not automatically entered into QuickBooks, you can enter the entire batch by simply double-clicking on the bolded group name in the **Memorized Transaction List**.

7
Customer and Vendor Relations

In this chapter, we will cover the following:

- ▸ Creating and transmitting custom batch letters
- ▸ Customizing invoices, purchase orders, and other documents
- ▸ Using the Collections Center
- ▸ Applying customer credit limits
- ▸ Creating and utilizing custom fields

Introduction

You will be able to use the recipes in this chapter to utilize non-accounting information to manage relationships with customers and vendors. These recipes include communication, management tools, and customizations of customer and vendor records.

The following table is the **Recipe Reference Card** for the keyboard shortcuts included in this chapter:

Customer Center	*Ctrl+J*

Creating and transmitting custom batch letters

Combine the database of **QuickBooks** with mail merging capabilities of **Microsoft Word** to quickly prepare custom batch letters for your customers, vendors, employees, or others. Use this recipe to create a completely customized letter, instead of just using the templates.

Getting ready

Make sure that the information for the desired recipients is included in the Customer List, Vendor List, or other appropriate list in QuickBooks. To quickly scan all customers for missing information, use the **Add/Edit Multiple List Entries** feature in the **Lists** menu.

How to do it...

1. Select **Customer Center** (*Ctrl + J*) | **Word** | **Customize Letter Templates** as shown in the following screenshot:

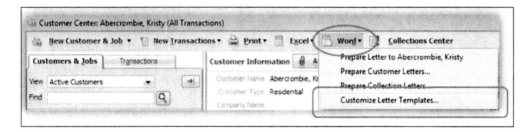

2. Select **Create a New Letter Template from Scratch**, and click on **Next**.

3. Choose a letter type, and enter a template name.

4. Click on the **Next** button. A Word document opens.

5. Prepare the letter as desired. To insert fields from the QuickBooks file, click on the **Add-Ins** tab.

6. With the cursor positioned where in the letter you wish to insert a field, make a selection from the **Insert My Company Fields** or **Insert Customer Name Fields** drop-down lists.

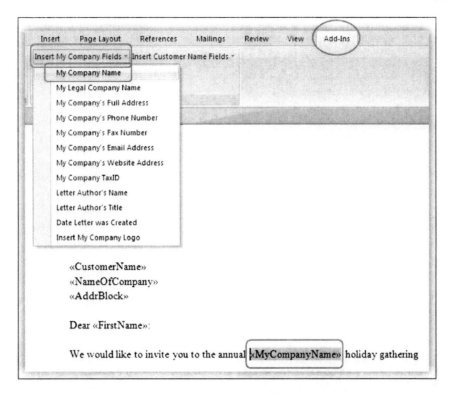

7. Repeat the preceding step as desired throughout the letter, and close the document.

8. In QuickBooks, click on the **Use Template** button, and then use the wizard to review and edit recipients. Select your new letter from the **Choose a Letter Template** list, and enter a name and title, if applicable.

9. The word document now contains a letter for each recipient. Edit any particular letter if desired. Save the file, or print the letters.

There's more...

The fastest way to prepare a separate one-page file to be e-mailed to each recipient is as follows:

1. Make sure you have **Adobe Standard**, or greater, installed on your computer.

2. Print to your Adobe PDF printer.

3. In Adobe Standard, select **Document | Extract Pages** as follows:

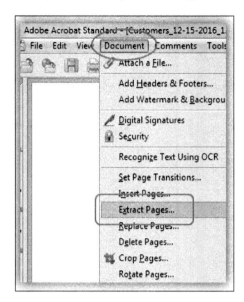

4. In the **To** field, enter the total number of pages in the document.

5. Check off **Extract Pages As Separate Files**, and click on **OK**:

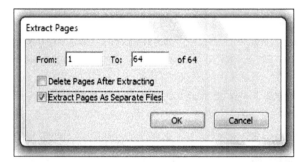

Customizing invoices, purchase orders, and other documents

This recipe will help you to design customer and vendor forms to include not only the desired transaction information, but also present a consistently branded look for your professional associates.

Documents with customizable templates are as follows:

> Sales Order
>
> Estimate
>
> Invoice
>
> Credit Memo
>
> Sales Receipt
>
> Statement
>
> Purchase Order
>
> Build Assembly

How to do it...

1. Select **Lists | Templates**.

2. Double-click on an existing template to edit it; or, from the **Templates** button, click on **Duplicate**. Select the transaction type, and double-click on **Duplicate** in the **Templates** list. At this point, no matter what your choice is for the preceding step, you should have a screen resembling the following screenshot:

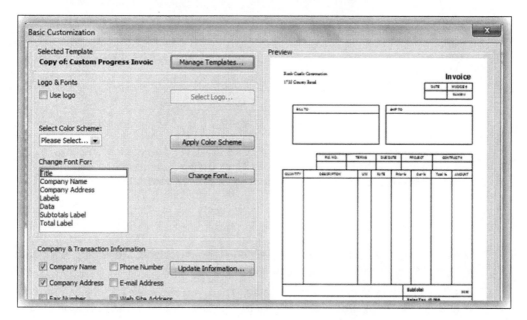

3. To customize the name of the template quickly, click on the **Manage Templates** button. Select a template name from the list on the left, if necessary, and then alter the entry in the **Template Name** field on the right-hand side of the screen, as follows:

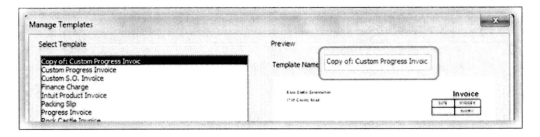

4. To easily control the fields included in your document, click on the **Additional Customization** button. Note the tabs across the top, and the document **Preview** that is always available on the right-hand side of the screen as follows:

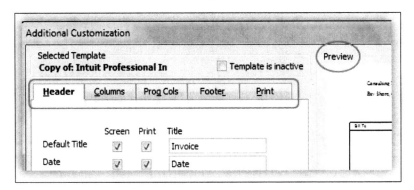

 The choices that appear in the **Prog Cols** tab depend on whether you have enabled the **Progress Invoicing** and **Sales Orders** features (select **Edit | Preferences | Company Preferences** followed by **Jobs & Estimates** or **Sales & Customers**, respectively).

5. To customize in a more detailed fashion, click on the **Layout Designer** button. The two major types of customizations possible in Layout Designer are editing objects and adding objects that you wish to include in the document.

6. To edit an existing object, select the object. Then, you can move the object, resize it, or click on the **Properties** button to change the **Text**, **Border**, or **Background** of the object, as shown in the following screenshot:

7. To insert a new object, click on the **Add** button, as shown in the following screenshot:

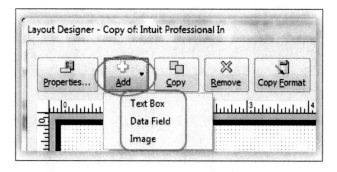

8. To add a label that is the same for all documents using this template, select **Text Box**.

9. To add information that is specific to the customer, item, or other QuickBooks-based piece of information, and that may change from document to document, select **Data Field**.

10. To add an image, such as a company logo, a COD symbol, a customer support icon, photo, or professional certification logos, click on **Image**, and browse to the location of the image already saved on your computer.

How it works...

Consider the template to be a different mechanism than the transaction itself. You may choose any invoice template on the **Create Invoices** screen, from the **Template** drop-down box, and the debits and credits of the transaction will not be affected.

Furthermore, templates can be exported and then imported into other QuickBooks files, as shown in the following screenshot:

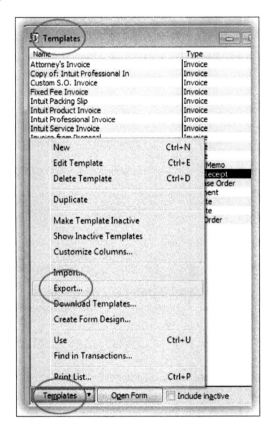

There's more...

Any custom field that you add (see the *Creating and utilizing custom fields* recipe, later in this chapter) appears automatically in the **Additional Customization** window, in the **Header** tab.

Using the Collections Center

The Collections Center report is structured somewhat differently from accounts receivable aging reports. Not only does it provide ready access to overdue balances, but it also is a means of getting in touch with the customers. This recipe provides the software portion of a collections process, ultimately to get cash at your door.

Getting ready

The Collections Center report is most useful on any day in which you have overdue customer invoices, or open customer invoices, due to be paid within the next 15 days. Therefore, to get the most from this recipe, make sure you have at least one saved invoice that meets one of those criteria.

How to do it...

1. Select **Customer Center** (*Ctrl+J*) | **Collections Center** as follows:

2. On the **Overdue** tab or the **Almost Due** tab, in the **Notes/Warnings** column, mouse over the icon to read any warnings related to that customer or job, as shown in the following screenshot:

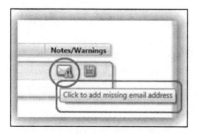

3. Take the opportunity to address warnings, such as the one about missing information, by clicking on the icon, which will cause the **Edit Customer**, or **Edit Job** window to open up, and following up with the customer to obtain that information.

4. In the same column, click on the **Notepad** icon to add a note to the customer record. The screen that opens has a different look but is synchronized with the **Notes** area in the **Edit Customer** window.

5. If an e-mail address has been entered into QuickBooks for a customer with an invoice listed in the Collections Center, a link automatically appears to facilitate an e-mail to that customer, with the invoice automatically attached as a PDF file, as shown in the following screenshot:

How it works...

The invoices in the Collections Center are automatically included, based on the **Due Date** field in individual invoices. The threshold for the **Almost Due** tab is 15 days from the current day.

To edit default language for the e-mails generated through the Collections Center, select **Edit | Preferences | Company Preferences | Send Forms**, and open the **Change default for** drop-down list. The **Overdue Invoices** and **Almost Due Invoices** options control the default language, as shown in the following screenshot:

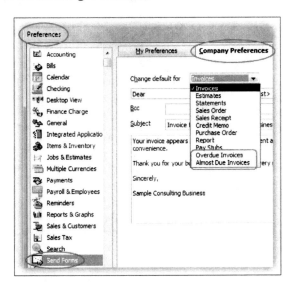

There's more...

The information in the Collections Center can be sorted by **Customer Name**, **Balance**, or **Days Overdue**, by clicking on the corresponding column header, as shown in the following screenshot:

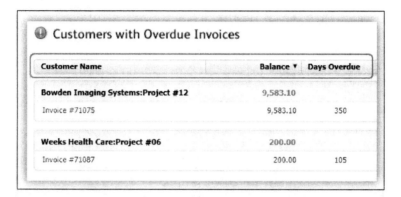

Applying customer credit limits

This recipe shows the power of just one field in QuickBooks. After entering the customer credit limit, you will be able to manage the services and products sold on credit, preclude certain users from overriding the customer credit limit, and stay on top of any customer balances that exceed their credit limit.

Getting ready

1. Select **Customer Center | Edit Customer**, or select **Edit Customer:Job | Payment Info | Credit Limit**. Enter in a credit limit.

2. Alternatively, if you wish to enter credit limits for many customers or jobs at once, select **Lists | Add/Edit Multiple List Entries**.

3. Click on the **Customize Columns** tab. In the **Available Columns** list, select **Credit Limit** and click on the **Add** button, as shown in the following screenshot:

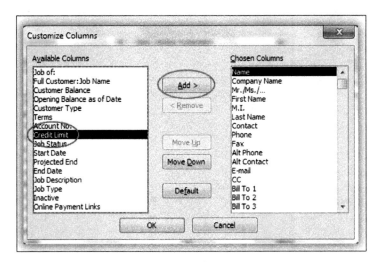

4. If desired, remove unneeded columns from the report by selecting a column header from the **Chosen Columns** list, and click on the **Remove** button.

5. After clicking on **OK**, enter credit limits for customers or for specific jobs. Click on the **Save Changes** button when done, as shown in the following screenshot:

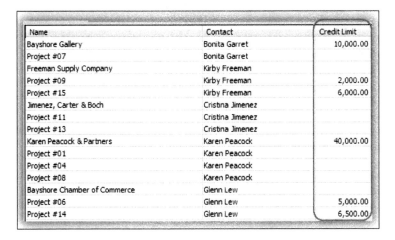

How to do it...

1. Create an invoice for a customer or job with a credit limit. If the new invoice amount plus the existing opening balance exceeds the credit limit, then upon clicking the **Save and Close** or **Save and New** button, you will see the following message:

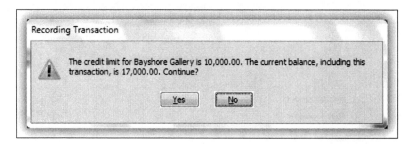

2. If the permissions for your login exclude the ability to override credit limits, you will see the following message instead:

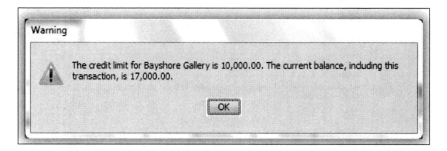

3. To preclude a user from overriding the credit limit, select a role for that user that includes the **None** setting for **Override Credit Limit**. Follow these steps:

   ❑ Select **Company | Users | Set Up Users and Roles | New**.

   ❑ In the **Available Roles** list, choose a role or multiple roles appropriate for the user, including the credit override setting. Click on **Add**, and when finished, click on **OK**, as shown in the following screenshot:

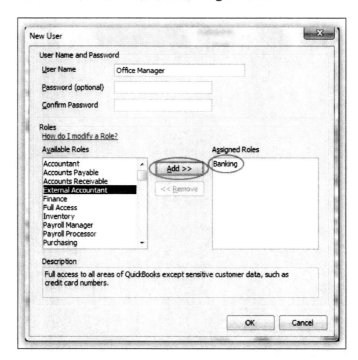

   ❑ To see the elements of each role in the **Users and Roles** list, click on the **View Permissions** button, select the user name, and click on the **Display** button, as shown in the following screenshot:

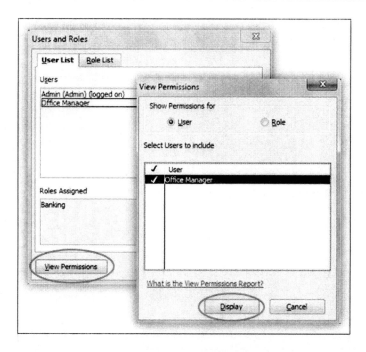

4. To see a report showing both credit limits and current balances, use the following steps:

- ❏ Select **Reports | List | Customer Phone List**.

- ❏ Click on **Customize Report**. In the **Display** tab, check off **Balance** and **Balance Total**, uncheck **Phone**, and check off **Credit Limit**.

- ❏ On the **Filters** tab, from the **Choose Filter** box, select **Credit Limit**, and set the credit limit to **1.00**.

- ❏ On the **Header/Footer** tab, add **Customer Credit Limits** as the **Report Title**, and click on **OK**:

Consulting Business
Customer Credit Limits
December 15, 2016

Customer	Balance	Balance Total	Credit Limit
Bayshore Gallery	0.00	17,043.20	10,000.00
Freeman Supply Company:Project #09	4,500.00	4,500.00	2,000.00
Freeman Supply Company:Project #15	2,000.00	2,000.00	6,000.00
Karen Peacock & Partners	0.00	0.00	40,000.00
Bayshore Chamber of Commerce:Projec...	0.00	0.00	5,000.00
Bayshore Chamber of Commerce:Projec...	0.00	0.00	6,500.00
Bowden Imaging Systems	0.00	10,933.10	10,000.00

- Visually scan the report for customers over their credit limit, or export the report to Excel.

- In the first blank column, to the right-hand side of the report, add a formula to distinguish **Customer** from their **Credit Limit**, as shown in the following screenshot:

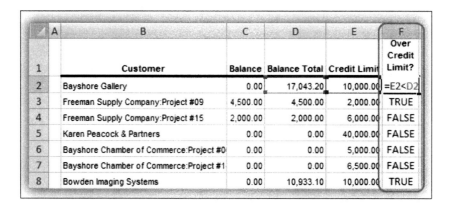

	A	B	C	D	E	F
						Over Credit Limit?
1		Customer	Balance	Balance Total	Credit Limit	
2		Bayshore Gallery	0.00	17,043.20	10,000.00	=E2<D2
3		Freeman Supply Company:Project #09	4,500.00	4,500.00	2,000.00	TRUE
4		Freeman Supply Company:Project #15	2,000.00	2,000.00	6,000.00	FALSE
5		Karen Peacock & Partners	0.00	0.00	40,000.00	FALSE
6		Bayshore Chamber of Commerce:Project #0	0.00	0.00	5,000.00	FALSE
7		Bayshore Chamber of Commerce:Project #1	0.00	0.00	6,500.00	FALSE
8		Bowden Imaging Systems	0.00	10,933.10	10,000.00	TRUE

5. Finally, add Filter to your report, and apply Filter to show only entries with the result **TRUE** in the **Over Credit Limit** column as follows:

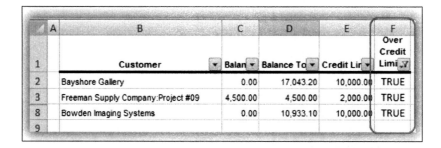

	A	B	C	D	E	F
						Over Credit Limi
1		Customer	Balan	Balance To	Credit Lir	
2		Bayshore Gallery	0.00	17,043.20	10,000.00	TRUE
3		Freeman Supply Company:Project #09	4,500.00	4,500.00	2,000.00	TRUE
8		Bowden Imaging Systems	0.00	10,933.10	10,000.00	TRUE
9						

Creating and utilizing custom fields

Use this recipe to create custom fields for customer and vendor information and then to use those fields in reports and templates, in order to gain more valuable summary information, communicate to your business associates, and take action for certain customers and vendors.

How to do it...

1. Select **Customer Center | Edit Customer:Job | Additional Info | Define Fields** or **Vendor Center | Edit Vendor | Additional Info | Define Fields**.

2. Enter a **Label** and add checkmarks in the **Cust** or **Vend** columns.

3. In the **What kind of data?** column, select the desired input mask, or create a custom drop-down list.

4. If you require this field in each transaction, or for each name in the **Customer:Job** or **Vendor** lists, indicate this with checkmarks in the **Trans** or **List** columns as follows:

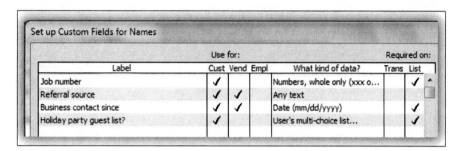

5. The completed Customer and Vendor windows now include your **Custom Fields**, including any drop-down boxes, as shown in the following screenshot:

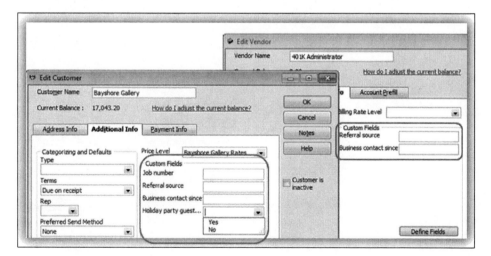

6. To use a custom field in a report, click on the **Customize** button, and on the **Display** tab, check off the column header. You may also be able to run a detailed report, and use the **Filters** tab, where the column header appears.

7. To use a custom field in a template, edit a template in the list, and click on the **Additional Customization** button. The column headers appear automatically on the **Header** tab. The custom fields are also automatically available in **Layout Designer**, when you click on the **Add** button, followed by the **Data** field.

8
Troubleshooting

In this chapter, we will cover the following recipes:

- ▸ Clearing stale undeposited funds
- ▸ Adjusting cash basis receivables or payables balances
- ▸ Writing off stale receivables
- ▸ Writing off stale payables
- ▸ Balancing the balance sheet
- ▸ Classifying unclassified transactions
- ▸ Reclassifying opening balance equity transactions
- ▸ Classifying uncategorized income or expenses
- ▸ Resolving opening balance discrepancies in bank reconciliations

Introduction

This chapter illuminates a number of accounting errors that are common in QuickBooks files, and enables you to resolve them.

The following table is the **Recipe Reference Card** for the keyboard shortcuts included in this chapter:

Find	Ctrl+F
Delete the line	Ctrl+Del
Save and close	Alt+A
Advance to the next field	Tab
Regress to the previous field	Shift+Tab
Customize the report	Alt+M
Change date range to All	A

Clearing stale undeposited funds

When the **Undeposited Funds** window includes customer payments, which you know have already been deposited, recorded, and reconciled, the **Income** or **Unearned Income** and **Undeposited Funds** accounts are overstated. You can use this recipe to efficiently combine the cleared deposit with the undeposited funds.

Getting ready

Verify that the appropriate bank account is reconciled for the period containing the stale undeposited funds. If not, this can be resolved simply by deleting the recorded deposit and recording the deposit of the undeposited funds.

How to do it...

1. With the **Find** tool (**Edit | Find** or *Ctrl+F*), use the **Amount** filter, along with the **Date** filter, if necessary, to bring up both the deposit and the customer payment already recorded.

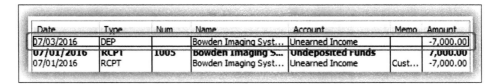

Date	Type	Num	Name	Account	Memo	Amount
07/03/2016	DEP		Bowden Imaging Syst...	Unearned Income		-7,000.00
07/01/2016	RCPT	1005	Bowden Imaging S...	Undeposited Funds		7,000.00
07/01/2016	RCPT		Bowden Imaging Syst...	Unearned Income	Cust...	-7,000.00

2. Open up the deposit, and click on the **Payments** button. Check off the appropriate transaction, and click on **OK** to add this to the deposit.

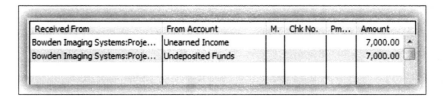

Received From	From Account	M.	Chk No.	Pm...	Amount
Bowden Imaging Systems:Proje...	Unearned Income				7,000.00
Bowden Imaging Systems:Proje...	Undeposited Funds				7,000.00

3. Click on the line item for the deposit originally on the screen, that is, the duplicate of the payment that you just added to this screen. Click on **Edit | Delete Line** (*Ctrl+Del*), and then **Save and Close** (*Alt+A*).

Received From	From Account	M.	Chk No.	Pm...	Amount
Bowden Imaging Systems:Proje...	Undeposited Funds				7,000.00

How it works...

The only way to directly delete an item added to Undeposited Funds is to delete the underlying customer payment or sales receipt. However, this is not advisable, because these transactions are typically accurate representations of a real-world activity.

Additionally, when the deposit was recorded, the related account duplicated the income or customer deposit from the original invoice or sales receipt.

Therefore, the deposit itself needs to be modified to simultaneously remove the duplicate offset account, and resolve the outstanding Undeposited Funds item.

There's more...

For a printable and memorizable list of all outstanding items in the Undeposited Funds account, open the **Undeposited Funds** ledger. Click on **Customize Report | Filters | Choose Filter | Cleared | No**. On the **Header/Footer** tab, in the **Report Title** field, enter Undeposited Funds, and click on **OK**.

Adjusting cash basis receivables or payables balances

Does your cash basis balance sheet show balance in your receivable or payables accounts? This recipe will take you through the two-step process of resolving these items:

- ▶ Locate them
- ▶ Adjust them

Getting ready

To find out which customers and vendors are responsible for your cash basis accounts receivable or accounts payable balances, respectively, run the following report:

1. Go to **Reports | Custom Reports | Summary**.
2. Set **Dates** to **All**. If you desire a cut-off date, leave the **From** field blank, and enter your cut-off date in the **To** field.
3. Set **Report Basis** to **Cash**.
4. Set **Display rows by** to **Customer** or **Vendor**.
5. Go to **Advanced**, and set **Display Rows** to **Non-zero**.

6. Go to the **Filters** tab, and set **Account** to **Accounts Receivable** (or **Accounts Payable**).

7. Go to the **Header/Footer** tab, and set **Report Title** to **Cash Basis A/R by Customer** or **Cash Basis A/P by Vendor**. The report total matches your balance sheet account total for the same cut-off date.

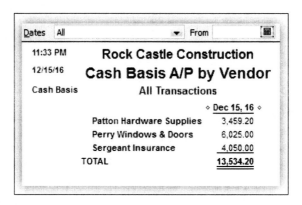

How to do it...

1. Double-click one of the account balances to reveal the detail, and remove the columns irrelevant to this effort.

2. Scan the activity for patterns, unusual items, or clues about the cash basis balance.

3. Gain an understanding of the transaction, and resolve the items by changing the accounts, changing a date, making a journal entry, noting that no adjustment is needed, or other action.

4. Refresh the report, and confirm either a zero balance or an appropriate cash basis balance.

How it works...

Some of the most likely patterns to scan for include the following:

▶ A **Balance** column, which keeps returning to 0.00, and then stops returning to 0.00:

11:48 PM | Rock Castle Construction
12/15/16 | **Custom Transaction Detail Report**
Cash Basis | All Transactions

Type	Date	Num	Debit	Credit	Balance
Bill Pmt -Check	08/05/2015	184	144.75		-144.75
Bill Pmt -Check	08/05/2015	184		144.75	0.00
Bill Pmt -Check	10/31/2015	214	1,287.00		-1,287.00
Bill Pmt -Check	10/31/2015	214		375.00	-912.00
Bill Pmt -Check	10/31/2015	214		912.00	0.00
Bill Pmt -Check	09/15/2016	395	4,998.95		-4,998.95
Bill Pmt -Check	09/15/2016	395		135.00	-4,863.95
Bill Pmt -Check	09/15/2016	395		4,823.95	-40.00
Bill Pmt -Check	09/15/2016	395		40.00	0.00
Bill	10/25/2016			840.00	840.00
Bill	10/25/2016			960.00	1,800.00
Bill	11/15/2016			810.00	2,610.00
Bill	11/18/2016			1,750.00	4,360.00
Bill	11/18/2016			75.00	4,435.00
Bill	11/20/2016			1,150.00	5,585.00
Bill	11/20/2016			600.00	6,185.00
Bill	11/20/2016			215.00	6,400.00

▶ An unusual transaction **Type:**

11:39 PM | Rock Castle Construction
12/15/16 | **Custom Transaction Detail Report**
Cash Basis | All Transactions

Type	Date	Num	Debit	Credit	Balance
Bill Pmt -Check	06/25/2016	338		1,109.15	6,109.15
Bill Pmt -Check	06/25/2016	338	1,109.15		5,000.00
Bill	07/30/2016	35698		405.00	5,405.00
Bill	07/30/2016	35698		349.50	5,754.50
Bill Pmt -Check	08/08/2016	371	1,214.89		4,539.61
Bill Pmt -Check	08/08/2016	371		1,214.89	5,754.50
Bill Pmt -Check	11/30/2016	472		656.23	6,410.73
Bill Pmt -Check	11/30/2016	472	656.23		5,754.50
Item Receipt	12/05/2016			87.50	5,842.00
Item Receipt	12/05/2016			3,000.00	8,842.00
Item Receipt	12/05/2016			162.00	9,004.00
Item Receipt	12/05/2016			209.70	9,213.70
Bill	12/05/2016	3847498	2,738.23		6,475.47
Bill	12/05/2016	3847498	985.76		5,489.71
Bill	12/05/2016	3847498	1,276.01		4,213.70
Bill Pmt -Check	12/05/2016	484		325.00	4,538.70
Bill Pmt -Check	12/05/2016	484	5,325.00		-786.30
Bill Pmt -Check	12/05/2016	484		2,738.23	1,951.93
Bill Pmt -Check	12/05/2016	484		985.76	2,937.69
Bill Pmt -Check	12/05/2016	484		1,276.01	4,213.70
Bill	12/15/2016	35698	405.00		3,808.70
Bill	12/15/2016	35698	349.50		3,459.20
Bill Pmt -Check	12/15/2016	503		405.00	3,864.20
Bill Pmt -Check	12/15/2016	503		349.50	4,213.70
Bill Pmt -Check	12/15/2016	503	754.50		3,459.20
Bill Pmt -Check	12/15/2016	512		400.00	3,859.20
Bill Pmt -Check	12/15/2016	512	400.00		3,459.20
Total			42,732.27	46,191.47	3,459.20

▶ A recurring figure in the **Balance** column. This lets you know that at least one culprit occurred before the recurrence began:

	11:39 PM 12/15/16 Cash Basis		**Rock Castle Construction** **Custom Transaction Detail Report** All Transactions			
⋄ Type ⋄	Date ⋄	Num ⋄	Debit ⋄	Credit ⋄	Balance ⋄	
Bill	12/05/2016	3847498	2,738.23		6,475.47	
Bill	12/05/2016	3847498	985.76		5,489.71	
Bill	12/05/2016	3847498	1,276.01		4,213.70	
Bill Pmt -Check	12/05/2016	484		325.00	4,538.70	
Bill Pmt -Check	12/05/2016	484	5,325.00		-786.30	
Bill Pmt -Check	12/05/2016	484		2,738.23	1,951.93	
Bill Pmt -Check	12/05/2016	484		985.76	2,937.69	
Bill Pmt -Check	12/05/2016	484		1,276.01	4,213.70	
Bill	12/15/2016	35698	405.00		3,808.70	
Bill	12/15/2016	35698	349.50		3,459.20	
Bill Pmt -Check	12/15/2016	503		405.00	3,864.20	
Bill Pmt -Check	12/15/2016	503		349.50	4,213.70	
Bill Pmt -Check	12/15/2016	503	754.50		3,459.20	
Bill Pmt -Check	12/15/2016	512		400.00	3,859.20	
Bill Pmt -Check	12/15/2016	512	400.00		3,459.20	
Total			42,732.27	46,191.47	3,459.20	

▶ A zero balance right before a transaction, which is also the aggregate balance sheet account balance:

	12:09 AM 12/15/16 Cash Basis		**Rock Castle Construction** **Custom Transaction Detail Report** All Transactions			
⋄ Type ⋄	Date ⋄	Num ⋄	Debit ⋄	Credit ⋄	Balance ⋄	
Bill Pmt -Check	07/31/2016	359	4,050.00		-4,050.00	
Bill Pmt -Check	07/31/2016	359		4,050.00	0.00	
Bill Pmt -Check	10/17/2016	424	0.00		0.00	
Bill Pmt -Check	10/31/2016	433	712.56		-712.56	
Bill Pmt -Check	10/31/2016	433		712.56	0.00	
Bill	12/15/2016			4,050.00	4,050.00	
Total			30,000.48	34,050.48	4,050.00	

There's more...

The most common reasons for a cash basis receivables or payable balance are:

▸ Payment date precedes bill or invoice date, and the report cut-off is between both the dates

▸ Offset account is a balance sheet account, and the bill or the invoice is unpaid

Writing off stale receivables

Making a journal entry to write off stale A/R in bulk is easy, but this makes it difficult to trace through the accounting records. The possible uses for more precise information include producing a trail for taxing authorities, internal or independent auditors, or banks. A separate spreadsheet may suffice, but it may be difficult to coordinate. This recipe focuses on straightforward ways to write off these balances in a detailed, but efficient fashion.

Getting ready

Have your criteria ready for which invoices are to be written off. The **A/R Aging Summary** report may help (**Reports | Customers & Receivables | A/R Aging Summary**).

To further analyze your oldest receivables:

1. Go to **Customize Report | Age through how many days?**, and type 360.

2. Go to **Filters | Choose Filter | Aging | >=**, and type 90.

3. Go to **Header/Footer**, add the text: Older Than 90 days to the **Report Title**, and click on **OK**.

How to do it...

To write off a stale receivable:

1. Go to the **Customers** page or **Home Page | Receive Payments**.

2. From the **Received From** drop-down box, select the appropriate customer. If applicable, select the particular job instead.

3. In the **Date** field, enter the effective date of the writeoff.

4. Click on the **Discount & Credits** button.

5. In the **Discount** and **Credits** pop-up window, fill in the amount to be written off, the writeoff account (generally **Bad Debt**), and the same class from the original invoice, if class tracking is used in the file:

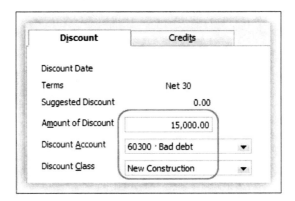

6. The completed screen should have 0.00 in the **Amount** and **Payment** fields. Include the amount written off in the **Discount** field:

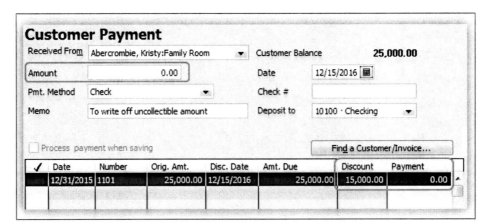

If an allowance for doubtful accounts is used against bad debt for writeoffs, then set up the **Allowance** account as an **Accounts Receivable** account type, and select the **Allowance** account from the drop-down box at the top of the **Customer Payments** screen. A set of journal entries can be used later, to remove the amounts from both **Accounts Receivable** and the **Allowance** account.

There's more...

This is the same procedure that can be used to record discounts, but the key is that an income or expense account must always be selected. This procedure is not appropriate for a balance sheet account to be selected, such as debiting a liability account while crediting A/R, or debiting the Allowance account while crediting A/R. This will cause a cash basis balance sheet report to be out of balance.

If that combination of debits and credits is essential, then use a journal entry instead. Then, apply the journal entry to the original invoice, by opening the invoice, and clicking the **Apply Credits** button.

When this recipe is used to write off receivables, **Act. Revenue** is reduced in the **Job Profitability Summary** report, and there is no effect on the **Item Profitability Summary** report. The same reporting results are attained if a journal entry is used to debit **Bad Debt Expense** and credit **Accounts Receivable**.

If a **Credit Memo** is used instead, **Act. Revenue** is reduced in the **Job Profitability Summary** report as well as the **Item Profitability Summary** report.

In order to increase the **Act. Cost** column in the **Job Profitability Summary** report instead, use the **Write Checks** screen in an unusual fashion: on the **Items** tab, use an **Other Charge** item called **Bad Debt** or **Writeoffs**. When you create this item, link it to the **Bad Debt Expense** account. On the **Write Checks** screen, be sure to enter the **Customer:Job** name as well as the writeoff amount.

On the **Expenses** tab, select **Accounts Receivable**, and enter the writeoff amount as a negative number, so that the total amount of the check equals 0. Be sure that the check bears no check number, and clear it in the next bank reconciliation.

This technique causes both the **Job Profitability** and **Item Profitability** reports to show the transaction as an expense, rather than as a reduction of revenue. It works because QuickBooks includes the **Write Check** transactions in the **Act. Cost** column of these reports.

Writing off stale payables

Making a journal entry to write off stale A/P in bulk is easy, but makes it difficult to trace through the accounting records. Possible uses for more precise information include producing a trail for taxing authorities, internal or independent auditors, or banks. A separate spreadsheet may suffice, but may be difficult to coordinate. This recipe focuses on straightforward ways to write off these balances in a detailed but efficient fashion.

Getting ready

Have your criteria ready for which bills are to be written off. The **A/P Aging Summary** report may help (**Reports | Vendors & Payables | A/P Aging Summary**).

To further analyze your oldest payables:

1. Go to **Customize Report | Age through how many days?**, and type 360.

2. Go to **Filters | Choose Filter | Aging | >=**, and type 90.

3. Go to **Header/Footer**, add the text: Older Than 90 days to the **Report Title**, and click on **OK**.

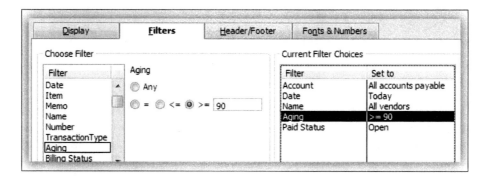

How to do it...

1. Go to **Vendors** or **Home Page | Pay Bills**.

2. Consider using the **Filter by** drop-down list to only show bills from a particular vendor, and consider using the **Sort by** drop-down list to organize the payables list by **Due Date**.

3. For one single vendor, check off the first bill to be written off.

4. Click on the **Set Discount** button.

5. In the **Discount** and **Credits** pop-up window, fill in the amount to be written off, the writeoff account (generally the same expense account as the original bill), and the same class from the original bill, if class tracking is used in the file:

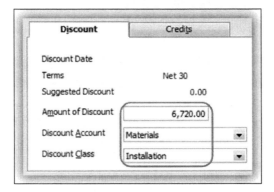

6. Click on **Done**, and proceed to the next bill for the same vendor.

7. Make sure the **Payment Date** field is the effective date of the write off.

8. The completed screen should have 0.00 in the **Amt. to Pay** field. Include the amount written off in the **Disc. Used** field:

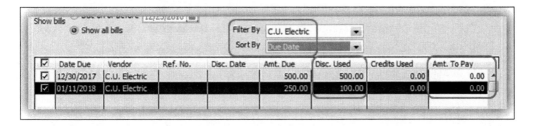

9. When the writeoffs for that vendor are complete, click on **Pay Selected Bills**, followed by **Pay More Bills** for additional writeoffs.

There's more...

The advantage of this recipe is that the transaction is created and applied to the bill in a single step. However, the drawback is that it does not appear in the **Job Profitability Summary** or the **Item Profitability Summary** reports. For that to occur, create a vendor credit instead, by using the **Enter Bills** screen, and clicking on the **Credit** button.

Then, use the **Items** tab to record the credit, using the same item that was used in the original bill. Additionally, use the **Customer:Job** field to apply the credit to a particular job.

For a partial writeoff, after the **Discount** and **Credits** window is closed, be sure to manually input 0.00 into the **Amt. to Pay** field. The default is to include the remaining balance in that field, and this recipe assumes that the current action is only to record writeoffs, not payments to vendors.

Balancing the balance sheet

How can a balance sheet get out of balance in a software program? If you're reading this recipe, you may have already seen for yourself that the impossible can happen. The following is a procedure to root out the transaction which is causing this phenomenon.

Getting ready

A balance sheet prepared on the cash basis can be out of balance if certain transactions were saved, for example if the **Discount** feature was used with a balance sheet account.

How to do it...

1. Open a **Balance Sheet Summary** report.
2. Click on the **Customize Report** button and in the **Dates** drop-down box, select **All**.
3. If the report is on the accrual basis, change the **Report Basis** to **Cash**.
4. In the **Display columns by** drop-down box, change the selection to **Year**, and click on **OK**.

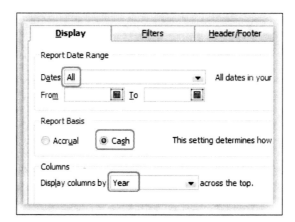

5. Look at the balance sheet, and identify the earliest year in which the balance sheet is out of balance.

6. Click on the **Customize Report** button. In the **From** and **To** fields, enter the beginning and ending dates of the year identified in the previous step.

7. In the **Display columns by** drop-down box, change the selection to **Month**, and click on **OK**.

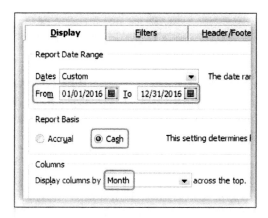

8. Look at the balance sheet, and identify the earliest month in which the balance sheet is out of balance.

9. Click on the **Customize Report** button. In the **From** and **To** fields, enter the beginning and ending dates of the month identified in the previous step.

10. In the **Display columns by** drop-down box, change the selection to **Week**, and click on **OK**.

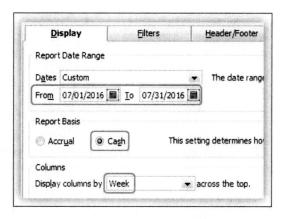

11. Look at the balance sheet, and identify the earliest week in which the balance sheet is out of balance.

12. Click on the **Customize Report** button. In the **From** and **To** fields, enter the beginning and ending dates of the week identified in the previous step.

13. In the **Display columns by** drop-down box, change the selection to **Day**, and click on **OK**.

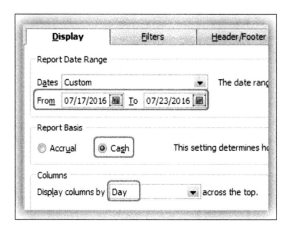

14. Look at the balance sheet, and identify the earliest day in which the balance sheet is out of balance:

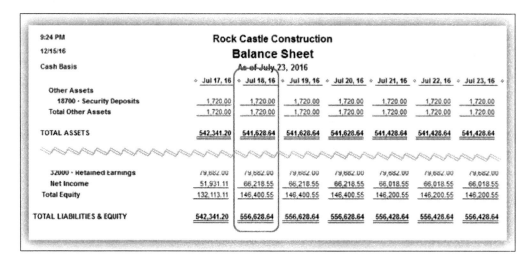

15. Run a transaction journal (**Reports | Accountant & Taxes | Journal**), limit the transactions to that day, and scan the report for the transaction responsible.

16. Delete the transaction which caused the imbalance, which is usually a **Customer Payment** or other **A/R** or **A/P** data entry screen, and make a journal entry instead, to cover the appropriate debit and credit.

There's more...

If the **Discount** feature was used to reclassify an **Accounts Receivable** balance to **Retainage Receivable,** make a journal entry to achieve the same **General Ledger** effect instead, and apply the transaction to the original invoice, by opening the invoice and using the **Apply Credits** button.

Classifying unclassified transactions

If class tracking is in use, then all income and expense transactions need to be assigned a class, in order to help ensure that the other class balances are accurate. It is easy to run a report of unclassified transactions, but more challenging to correct them efficiently. This recipe includes two means of doing so.

Getting ready

1. Go to **Reports | Company & Financial | Profit & Loss Unclassified**.

2. Set the date range as appropriate.

   If you have the **Client Data Review** feature available in **Accountant Edition**, then proceed to the next step:

3. Note the accounts which contain unclassified transactions. Consider printing this report, or, in a dual-monitor environment, expanding the QuickBooks application, by clicking on **View | Multiple Windows**, and arranging this report on only one monitor.

How to do it...

1. If you do not have the **Client Data Review** feature available in the **Accountant Edition**, the following keyboard shortcuts will help you efficiently add a class to the unclassified transactions:

   ❑ Press and hold *Tab* to quickly move through the fields above the report: **Dates, From, To, Columns,** and **Sort by**.

   ❑ In the first account balance, press *Enter*.

   ❑ In the detail report, press and hold *Tab* to quickly move through the fields above the report: **Dates, From, To, Columns,** and **Sort by**.

   ❑ Press *Enter* to open the first transaction in the list.

- ❑ Press *Tab* to advance to the **Class** field. If you go too far, press *Shift+Tab* to move back to the previous field.

- ❑ In the **Class** field, start typing the name of the appropriate class.

- ❑ Once it appears, press *Alt+A* to Save and Close.

An additional shortcut:

If the screen is the **Write Checks**, or **Enter Bills**, or **Enter Credit Card Charges** screen, then *Alt+X* or *Alt+M* reduces the number of *Tab* strokes necessary to get to the **Class** field. This is because *Alt+X* jumps to the **Expenses** tab, and *Alt+M* jumps to the **Items** tab:

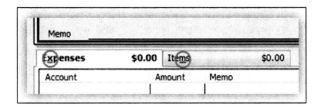

If you are uncertain as to the appropriate class for this transaction, press *Ctrl+Q* to run a QuickReport on that customer or vendor.

Then quickly add the **Class** field to the report by pressing *Alt+M* (**Customize Report**), and checking off the **Class** column.

When in the **Class** field, if you want to see a complete list of classes without slowing down to pick up the mouse and click on it, press *Alt+down* arrow. Then, as usual, start typing the name of the desired class, and press *Alt+A* to Save and Close.

2. If you do have the **Client Data Review** feature available in the **Accountant Edition**:

- ❑ Go to **Accountant | Client Data Review**. Start the review, and click on **Reclassify Transactions**.

- ❑ In the left-hand margin, set the date range and the report basis as appropriate.

- ❑ From the **View** drop-down box, select **Profit & Loss Accounts**.

- ❑ Select the first account noted in the **Unclassified Transactions** report.

- ❑ On the right-hand side of the screen, set **Show Transactions** to **All**, and check off **Include Journal Entries**.

- ❑ Click on the **Class** header, so that an upward-pointing triangle appears. This sorts the list by **Class**, placing the unclassified transactions at the top of the list.

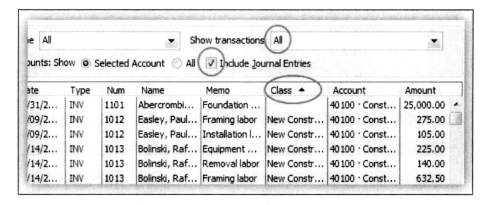

☐ Select the checkboxes next to each of the transactions, which need to be assigned the same class, and at the bottom of the screen indicate the appropriate class.

☐ Click on **Reclassify**, and repeat this recipe.

How it works...

Only certain transactions can be assigned a class using the **Client Data Review**. If this poses a stumbling block for you, then follow the alternate procedure, and learn the keyboard shortcuts, which make the **Profit & Loss Unclassified** report easy to get through quickly.

Reclassifying Opening Balance Equity transactions

Although reclassifying the **Opening Balance Equity** transactions is straightforward, this recipe also includes a procedure for avoiding this problem in the first place.

How to do it...

1. From the Home page or **List** menu, open the **Chart of Accounts** (*Ctrl+A*).

2. Start typing quickly the phrase `Opening Balance Equity`, until QuickBooks jumps to that account, or simply look for it in the list.

3. Run a QuickReport (right-click the account, and select **QuickReport** or press *Ctrl+Q*).

4. If the date range is not **All**, then without clicking on anything, press the letter *A* to switch the highlighted **Date** field to **All**.

5. Open the transaction, and assign the appropriate account, likely **Retained Earnings** or partner ownership accounts:

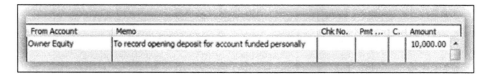

How it works...

QuickBooks includes various opportunities to enter an opening balance, notably when a new company file, account, or item is created. In certain screens, such as bank accounts and inventory items, an opening balance causes an entry into the **Opening Balance Equity** account:

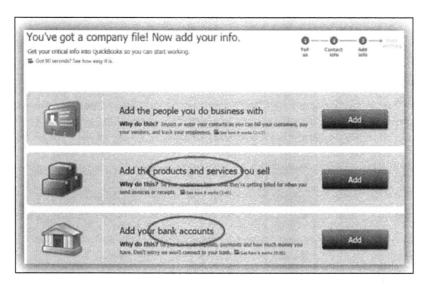

This screenshot, encountered during the interview process, is the gateway to entering opening balances, which might cause the Opening Balance Equity account to come into play.

The following screenshot is displayed after the above "products and services" **Add** button is clicked, and the screenshot for the bank accounts is similar:

The **Opening Balance** field, or in the case of **Inventory Parts**, the **Total Value** field as shown, is the culprit. Use the **Inventory Adjustment** screen instead, where you can select the appropriate offset account from a drop-down list.

For bank accounts, create a deposit instead to record the opening balance directly to the **Retained Earnings** or partner ownership accounts.

If there are many such transactions and multiple partners, it is more efficient to use the procedure recommended by QuickBooks, namely, one single journal entry, mass-reclassifying the Opening Balance Equity account to the appropriate partner ownership accounts.

There's more...

The **Client Data Review** feature can also be used to move transactions out of **Opening Balance Equity**. However, not all transactions may be accessible in this feature to be reclassified.

Classifying uncategorized income or expenses

The Uncategorized Income and Uncategorized Expense accounts are created by QuickBooks automatically, when opening balances are entered for customers or vendors. Use this recipe to reclassify these balances, and to avoid this problem in the first place.

Getting ready

If you are not going to use the Client Data Review tool available in the Accountant Edition, then get ready by running the following report of all transactions in these accounts:

1. Go to **Reports | Custom Reports | Transaction Detail**.
2. Set the date range as appropriate.
3. Go to **Filters**. In the **Choose Filter** box, select **Account**; it may be already selected by default.
4. In the drop-down box, select **Multiple accounts...**, located at the top of the list.
5. Check off the **Uncategorized Income** and **Uncategorized Expense** accounts, and click on **OK**.
6. Optional: On the **Header/Footer** tab, in the **Report Title** field, substitute a meaningful report header for **Custom Transaction Detail Report**.

How to do it...

To reclassify balances:

Without the Client Data Review tool, simply use the previous report, and either open each transaction and enter the appropriate account, or create a journal entry to reclassify the balances in bulk.

Alternatively, use the Client Data Review's Reclassify tool as described earlier in this chapter to reclassify balances of these accounts. The only difference from the earlier recipe is that the **Account** field at the bottom of the screen will be used, rather than the **Class field**:

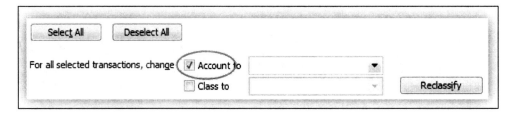

To avoid the problem:

Rather than entering opening balances for customers in an **Opening Balance** field, create an item linked to the **Retained Earnings** account, and enter an invoice for each customer.

The advantage of this approach is an accurate and transparent trail in the General Ledger, but the disadvantage is that it takes more time than entering in the balances and doing a bulk reclassification.

How it works...

Because QuickBooks is a double-entry accounting system, entering an opening balance for a customer or vendor, as shown in the following screenshot, actually causes an entry into the General Ledger:

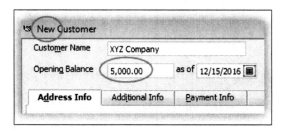

The information may be entered in bulk during the file setup process:

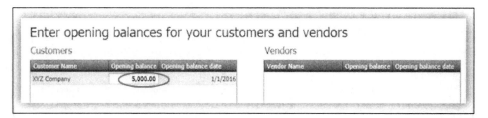

Regardless of which of the previous screens is used, the General Ledger accounts affected are Accounts Receivable and Uncategorized Income, in the case of customer balances, and in the case of vendor balances, the accounts are Uncategorized Expense and Accounts Payable.

There's more...

The customer and vendor opening balances can also be entered in bulk using the **Lists | Add/Edit Multiple List Entries** feature. To add the **Opening Balance** column to the screen, click on the **Customize Columns** button, and add either **Customer Balance** or **Vendor Balance**, as appropriate.

Resolving opening balance discrepancies in bank reconciliations

You're reconciling a bank or credit card account, and there is still a difference. Both your deposits and other credits ,and your checks and payments totals match the bank statement totals, and you're confident that you typed your Ending Balance correctly. The likely culprit? A **Beginning Balance** that does not match the bank statement, and in QuickBooks, this is not a data entry field. This recipe details how to resolve this discrepancy quickly.

How to do it...

The stages of troubleshooting this problem are to locate it, fix it, and finally re-reconcile the account to wrap it up. The following recipe shows each step in the process.

1. Find and fix:

    □   Run the **Previous Reconciliation Discrepancy Report: Reports | Banking | Reconciliation Discrepancy**, and select the appropriate account.

    □   Note the transactions included in the report, in particular the **Type of Change** and **Effect of Change** columns.

    □   To gain more information about deleted transactions, go to **Reports | Accountant & Taxes | Voided/Deleted Transactions Detail**.

    □   Once you determine the correct transaction, enter it into QuickBooks or fix an existing transaction.

2. Re-reconcile

> The most efficient solution is to re-open the **Reconcile** window, and check off the corrected transactions. Although this does not correct the opening balance per se, it will move the difference to 0.00, and once this reconciliation is complete, the next opening balance will be correct.

3. A less efficient, but more exacting solution, is to undo reconciliations for the previous months (**Banking | Reconcile | Undo Previous Reconciliation**) through to the period in which the corrected transactions actually cleared, and redo the reconciliations. If you choose this option, consider the following techniques for a highly efficient re-reconciliation:

    □   Prior to undoing the previous reconciliations, print the original PDFs, or save them to your computer.

❑ Upon re-reconciling each month, check off the **Hide transactions after the statement's end date** checkbox.

❑ Click on **Mark All**.

❑ Using the previously printed or saved bank reconciliation as your guide, simply uncheck the uncleared transactions. These are generally fewer in number than the cleared transactions:

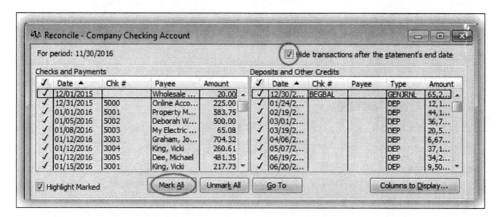

❑ Reconcile and repeat until the reconciliations are up to date.

How it works...

The most common reasons for an opening balance discrepancy are:

▸ A user clicked on the "cleared" checkmark in the register, and ignored the pop-up warning message

▸ A user changed the bank or credit card account in the original transaction, even if it gets changed back to the correct account

▸ A user deleted a cleared transaction

There's more...

Occasionally, the **Previous Reconciliation Discrepancy Report** does not display the desired information. A backup plan is to compare the two versions of previous reconciliations, and identify the differences in cleared numbers:

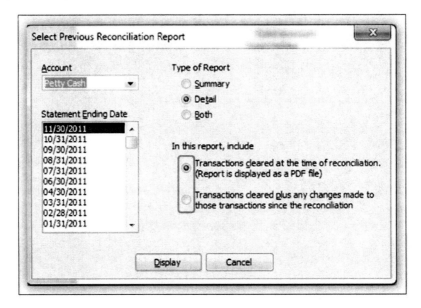

9

Keyboard Shortcuts

In this chapter, we will cover the following recipes:

- ▸ Using the *Ctrl* key shortcuts with lists
- ▸ Using the *Ctrl* key shortcuts with transactions
- ▸ Using the *Alt* key shortcuts
- ▸ Using date shortcuts
- ▸ Using other shortcut techniques

Introduction

By the end of this chapter, the expert QuickBooks user will be positioned to dramatically increase the speed of those QuickBooks tasks that are most important and common to you. Use the relevant shortcuts included in these recipes, but transfer the underlying techniques to other areas of QuickBooks to suit your working style.

Using the Ctrl key shortcuts with lists

Some *Ctrl* key shortcuts are the same as in any program on a Windows machine, and some are specific to the QuickBooks environment. To activate the shortcuts in these recipes, use the *Ctrl* key on your keyboard.

Getting ready

Ctrl shortcuts may produce different results, depending on what screen is currently displayed in QuickBooks. For example, *Ctrl+N* produces a new account, new customer, or new vendor, depending on what list is displayed when the shortcut is used.

How to do it...

Chart of Accounts:

- Press *Ctrl+A* to open the Chart of Accounts
- To quickly get to a specific account, start typing the account name or number
- To edit the account, press *Ctrl+E*
- To run a QuickReport instead, press *Ctrl+Q*
- To create a new account instead, press *Ctrl+N*
- To delete an unused account, press *Ctrl+D*

Common combinations include:

- **Create a new account**: Press *Ctrl+A*, followed by *Ctrl+N*
- **Edit an existing account**: Press *Ctrl+A*, type the name or number of the account, and press *Ctrl+E*
- **Run a QuickReport for an account**: Press *Ctrl+A*, type the name or number of the account, and press *Ctrl+Q*

Task	Shortcut	Mnemonic
Open the Chart of Accounts	Ctrl+A	A = Accounts
Navigate to an account	Quickly type name or number of account	
Edit a selected account	Ctrl+E	E = Edit
Run a QuickReport for a selected account	Ctrl+Q	Q = Quick
New account	Ctrl+N	N = New
Delete an unused account	Ctrl+D	D = Delete

Customer Center:

- ▸ Press *Ctrl+J*
- ▸ Use the same combinations as for the Chart of Accounts shortcuts to create a new customer, edit an existing customer or job, run a QuickReport for a customer or job, or delete a customer or job with no transactions

Memorized Transaction List:

- ▸ Press *Ctrl+T*

There's more...

Additional lists

The **New, Edit, Delete, QuickReport,** and navigational shortcuts described in the previous section also work with the following lists:

- ▸ **Vendor Center**
- ▸ **Other Names** list
- ▸ **Item** list
- ▸ **Class** list
- ▸ **To Do** list
- ▸ **Other** lists in the **Lists** menu or elsewhere in QuickBooks

A number of *Ctrl* shortcuts are displayed within QuickBooks menus.

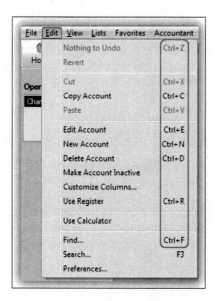

Using the Ctrl key shortcuts with transactions

Use the shortcuts included in this recipe during the data entry process. Similar to the *Ctrl* key shortcuts for list screens, some shortcuts also work in the general Windows environment and in other programs, and some are specific to the QuickBooks environment.

How to do it...

1. Open data entry screens.

Screen	Shortcut	Mnemonic
Invoice	Ctrl+I	I = Invoice
Write Checks	Ctrl+W	W = Write
Register	Ctrl+R	R = Register

2. Cut, copy, and paste:

   □ Highlight the desired text. The easiest way to do this is to use the *Tab* key until you reach the appropriate field. For most fields, the entirety of the text is automatically highlighted.

   □ Use the shortcut as indicated:

Task	Shortcut	Mnemonic
Cut	Ctrl+X	Proximity to "paste" makes the cut-paste combination convenient
Copy	Ctrl+C	C = Copy
Paste	Ctrl+V	Proximity to "copy" makes the copy-paste combination convenient

3. Common combinations include the following:

   □ **Cut-paste**: Press *Ctrl* + *X*, followed by pressing *Ctrl* + *V*

   □ **Copy-paste**: Press *Ctrl* + *C*, followed by pressing *Ctrl* + *V*

4. Insert and delete lines:

   □ Position the cursor on a part of the data entry screen with multiple lines, as opposed to discrete fields separated from the rest of the form.

For Write Checks, Enter Bills, or Enter Credit Card Charges, click on the area indicated in the following screenshot, on either the **Expenses** tab or the **Items** tab:

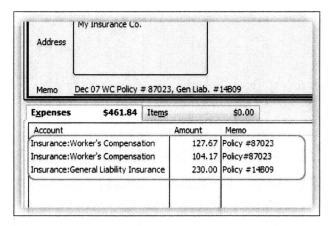

For Make Deposits, click on the area indicated in the following screenshot:

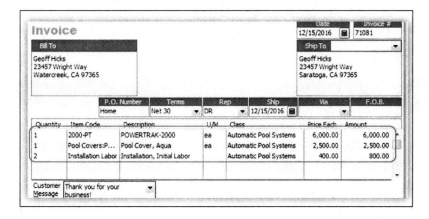

For Invoices, Sales Receipts, Sales Orders, Estimates, Credit Memos, and Purchase Orders, click on the area indicated in the following screenshot:

To insert a row above the row in which the cursor is located, press *Ctrl + Insert*.

To delete the entire row in which the cursor is located, press *Ctrl +Delete*. Please note: this is not *Ctrl +D*, which deletes the entire transaction. The *Delete* key is the one on your keyboard which says *Delete* or *Del*.

 Other data entry screens contain multiple rows as well. Examples include the **Weekly Timesheet** and the **Adjust Quantity/Value on Hand** screen.

Common combinations include the following:

- ▶ Add an entry above the current line: After pressing *Ctrl + Ins*, type your information as desired. Then, tap the Tab key, enter in more information as desired, tap the *Tab* key, and repeat until complete.

- ▶ Add an entry with a field containing a drop-down box, above the current line: Press *Ctrl+Ins*, followed by pressing *Alt+*down arrow key, to open the drop-down box for that field. You can use the arrow keys to select list item, and press the *Tab* key to move to the next field.

- ▶ Remove several lines: Hold down the *Ctrl* key, and tap the *Del* key repeatedly. Each time you tap *Del*, the current line is removed from the data entry screen. Release the *Ctrl* key when complete.

Task	Shortcut
Insert a line	Ctrl+Ins
Delete a line	Ctrl+Del

 Not all data entry screens with multiple rows are compatible with *Ctrl +Ins* and *Ctrl+Del*. Examples include **Pay Bills** (use the **Filter By** drop-down box instead), the check register (double-click a split transaction to use the **Write Checks** screen instead), and **Receive Payments** (be sure to check off only the applicable invoices).

Using the Alt key shortcuts

The underlying power of the *Alt* key shortcuts detailed in this recipe is that it activates the underlined letter in any menu items or buttons as if you had clicked on that item or object with the mouse.

The *Alt* key shortcuts are highly context-specific, and it takes time to see which letter is underlined. At first, it doesn't feel like a true shortcut at all! Therefore, only memorize the most frequently-used *Alt* shortcuts, and add to your repertoire gradually over time.

The power to use the *Alt* key to activate the underlined letters is available in the Windows operating system itself, as well as most computer programs. This technique has a reach far greater than the QuickBooks application!

Getting ready

The *Alt* shortcuts are only effective with the items displayed on the screen at the moment you press the *Alt* key. Therefore, in order to get ready to use these shortcuts, be sure that you have the appropriate screen displayed.

How to do it...

1. Run financial reports:

   ❑ **Balance Sheet**: Press *Alt+R+F+B*

Task	Alt Shortcut
Activate the **Reports** menu	R
Activate the **Company and Financial** submenu	F
Activate the **Balance Sheet Standard** report	B

   ❑ **Profit & Loss**: Press Alt+R+F+S.

Task	Alt Shortcut
Activate the **Reports** menu	R
Activate the **Company and Financial** submenu	F
Activate the **Profit & Loss Standard** report	S

Note the underlined letters in the following screenshot of the menu, which reflects these shortcuts:

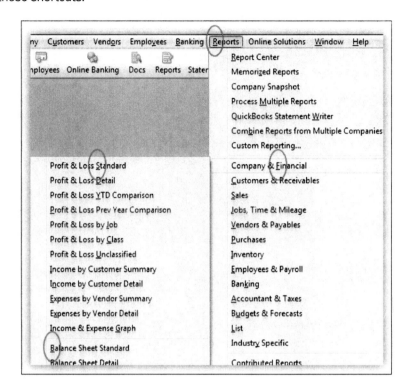

- **Accounts Receivable Aging**: Press *Alt+R+C+A*.

Task	Alt Shortcut
Activate the **Reports** menu	R
Activate the **Customers & Receivables** submenu	C
Activate the **A/R Aging Summary** report	A

The following screenshot illustrates the previous shortcuts in action:

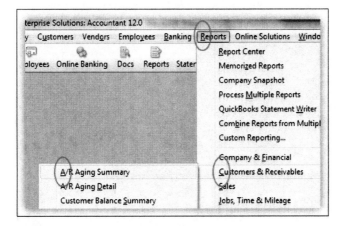

   ❑   **Accounts Payable Aging**: Press *Alt+R+V+A*.

Task	Alt Shortcut
Activate the **Reports** menu	R
Activate the **Vendors & Payables** submenu	V
Activate the **A/P Aging Summary** report	A

The following screenshot illustrates the previous shortcuts in action:

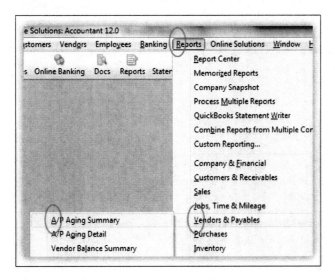

2. Jump to the relevant data entry fields:

    ❑   In the **Write Checks**, **Enter Bills**, or **Enter Credit Card Charges** screen, press *Alt+X* to jump to the **Expenses** tab, or *Alt+M* to jump to the **Items** tab.

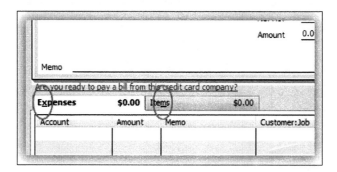

3. In the **Write Checks** screen, press *Alt+K* to jump to the **Bank Account** field. This is especially helpful if you've filled out the entire screen, only to realize that the incorrect bank account was selected

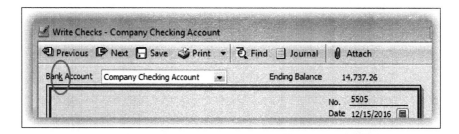

4. In the **Sales Order**, **Estimates**, **Invoice**, **Sales Receipt**, and **Credit Memo** screens, press *Alt+J* to jump to the **Customer:Job** field. This is especially helpful if you've filled out the entire screen, only to realize that the incorrect customer or job was selected:

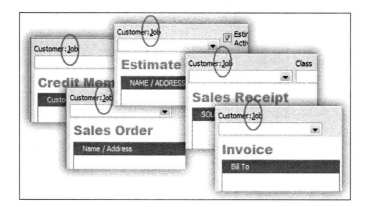

The following table shows some additional *Alt* shortcuts that facilitate the flow of the data entry in a number of screens throughout QuickBooks:

Screen	Task	Alt Shortcut
Write Checks, **Enter Bills**, or **Enter Credit Card Charges**	Jump to the **Expenses** tab	X
Write Checks, **Enter Bills**, or **Enter Credit Card Charges**	Jump to the **Items** tab	M
Write Checks	Jump to **Bank Account** field	K
Sales Order, **Estimates**, **Invoice**, **Sales Receipt**, and **Credit Memo**	Jump to **Customer:Job** field	J

5. Activate the buttons on data entry screens, reports, and dialog boxes:

    ❏ On most of the data entry screens, press *Alt+A* for **Save & Close** or *Alt+S* for **Save & New**:

    ❏ On most of the data entry screens, press *Alt+P* for **Previous**, and *Alt+N* for **Next**. This is a hidden shortcut, and is effective regardless of whether the **P** and **N** are underlined or not.

    ❏ On most reports, press *Alt+M* for the **Customize** button, *Alt+X* for the **Excel** button, and *Alt+P* for the **Collapse** or **Expand** button:

6. In the **Modify Report** pop-up box, press *Alt+D*, *Alt+F*, *Alt+H*, or *Alt+N* to activate each of the four tabs across the top.

7. In the **Display** tab:

   ❑ Press *Alt+M* or *Alt+T* to jump to the **From** or **To** fields, respectively.

   ❑ Press *Alt+U* or *Alt+S* to change the report basis.

   ❑ Press *Alt+P*, *Alt+Y*, *Alt+W*, or *Alt+O* to add subcolumns to the report.

   ❑ If the report that you generated is a **Profit & Loss** report, additional options are available, including *Alt+R* to add a Year-to-Date sub-column.

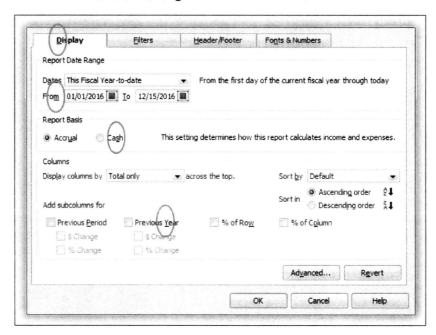

Common combinations include:

   ❑ **Change to a cash basis report**: Press *Alt+M+S*, followed by pressing *Ctrl+Enter* (activates the **OK** button)

   ❑ **Add the previous year to a report**: Press *Alt+M+Y*, followed by pressing *Ctrl+Enter* (activates the **OK** button)

   ❑ **Export a report to Excel**: Press *Alt+X+N+X*

   ❑ **Open a QuickBooks file**: Press *Alt+N*

❑ **Save a change to a transaction affecting Retained Earnings**: Press *Alt+A*, followed by pressing *Alt+Y*, and *Alt+O*

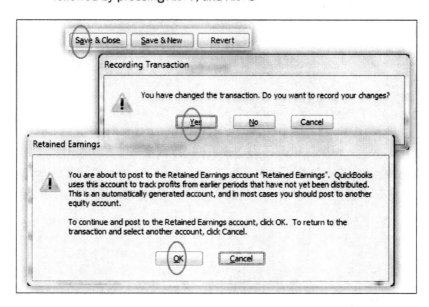

The following table shows some additional *Alt* shortcuts that facilitate the flow of the data entry in a number of screens throughout QuickBooks:

Screen	Task	Alt Shortcut
Most data entry screens	Save and close	A
Most data entry screens	Save and new	S
Most data entry screens	Previous transaction	P
Most data entry screens	Next transaction	N
Customize Report screen	Activate each of the four tabs across the top	D, F, H, N
Customize Report screen	Jump to the **From** or **To** fields	M, T
Customize Report screen	Change the report basis to **Accrual** or **Cash**	U, S
Customize Report screen	Add **Previous Period, Previous Year**, **% Row, % Column, Year-to-Date**	P, Y, W, O, R

There's more...

Open data entry screens, which do not have a *Ctrl* key shortcut.

▸ **Enter bills**: *Alt+O+B*
▸ **Pay bills**: *Alt+O+P*

▸ **Receive payment**: *Alt+U+Y*

▸ **Record deposit**: *Alt+B+D*

An *Alt* shortcut which is independent of any letter being underlined, is *Alt+F4*. This closes the QuickBooks application, and in fact, closes whatever application you have open on a Windows machine, if that application has the focus when the shortcut is pressed.

When using the *Alt* shortcuts, there is no need to hold down the *Alt* key as there is with the *Ctrl* key. Simply press the keys in sequence.

Using date shortcuts

As you gain mastery with keyboard shortcuts, it soon becomes painfully apparent how much the on-screen calendar in the QuickBooks date fields slow you down. Use the shortcuts in this recipe to speed through the **Date** field anywhere it appears in QuickBooks, from a data entry screen to a report to the Create Statements tool.

Getting ready

For most of the date shortcuts to be effective, the field needs to be completely highlighted. Instead of manually highlighting the field with the mouse, simply use the *Tab* key to navigate your way through each field. The *Tab* key causes the **Date** field to be fully highlighted automatically.

How to do it...

1. For certain dates there is no *Ctrl* or *Alt* requirement with date shortcuts. Simply press the key indicated:

Date	Shortcut	Mnemonic
Today	T	T = today
End of the month	H	H = the end of the word "month"
End of the year	R	R = the end of the word "year"
Increase the day by 1	+	
Decrease the day by 1	-	

2. Common combinations include:

   ❑ Tomorrow: *T +*

   ❑ Yesterday: *T -*

3. Other dates when you need to enter a date manually because it doesn't fall near any of the shortcut dates provided above:

   ❑ If the date is in the current year, simply type the date in the form "mmdd" and move on. For example, for a March 15 date, type 0315. When you move on to another field, QuickBooks automatically adds the slashes and the current year, for example 03/15/2012:

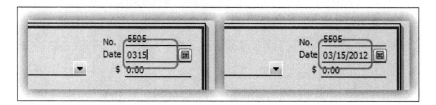

   ❑ If the date is not in the current year, type the date in the form "mmddyy." For example, 03/15/11. When you exit the field, QuickBooks automatically adds the slashes and the full year, for example 03/15/2011:

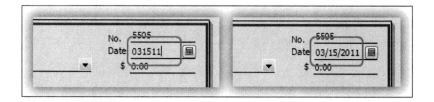

There's more...

A comprehensive list of date shortcuts is available online in many places, but the shortcuts included in this recipe are the most commonly used.

Using other shortcut techniques

There are other shortcut techniques that can be used alone, or, more powerfully, in combination with *Ctrl* and *Alt* to save a great deal of time, and keep your thought process-focused on your work, rather than on the interface.

Spacebar

When a button, checkbox, or option button has the focus, use the spacebar to activate the object, as if you had clicked on it.

If the desired button is not highlighted, and there is no underlined letter (or else the *Alt* shortcut might be desirable), use the *Tab* key to move the focus to the desired object, and then use the spacebar to activate the object.

1. The *spacebar* combination shown in the following screenshot is explained as follows:

    ❑ Customize the report, and add a column for last year, with the **$ Change**:

    ❑ Press *Alt+M*, followed by *Alt+Y*. Press the down arrow on your keyboard, followed by the spacebar.

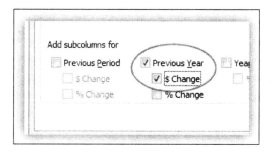

2. The *spacebar* combination shown in the following screenshot is explained as follows:

    ❑ Customize the report, and add a filter to only include transactions equal to $1,000.

    ❑ Press *Alt+M*, followed by *Alt+F*. Press the down arrow to highlight the word **Amount**, press the *Tab* key until the equal sign is indicated, press the spacebar to select the equal sign; press the *Tab* key until you can type in the amount of 1000.

    ❑ Or, use the **Find** feature to list transactions equal to $1,000.

    ❑ Press *Ctrl+F* to activate the **Find** feature. If you're not on the **Advanced** tab already, press *Alt+A*. Press the down arrow to highlight the word **Amount**, and then press the *Tab* key until the equal sign is indicated. Press the spacebar to select the equal sign, press the *Tab* key until you can type in the amount of 1000.

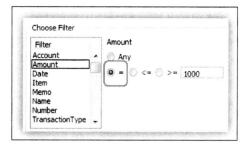

Esc

Press *Esc* to close whatever screen is on top in QuickBooks, be it a data entry screen, report, or dialog box that you wish to exit without entering a response.

Not only does this save time, but it saves you from closing the entire QuickBooks application when you only meant to close a report...

To close several windows, hit *Esc* several times. To close all open windows in QuickBooks, use the *Alt+W+A* combination (**Window | Close** All).

Tab

Press the *Tab* key to advance to the next field, be it in a data entry screen or report setting.

To quickly move backward to a previous field without having to grab the mouse, press *Shift+Tab*.

10

Integration with Excel

In this chapter, we will cover the following:

- ▶ Combining reports from multiple entities
- ▶ Setting up reports for optimal exporting
- ▶ Updating exported reports
- ▶ Using Excel to edit lists hyperefficiently

Introduction

After following the recipes in this chapter, the reader will be able to use advanced integration features with Microsoft Excel, including preparing combined reports from multiple QuickBooks files, setting up reports for optimal analysis once exported into Excel, and moving information from Excel into QuickBooks.

Combining reports from multiple entities

Getting ready

Make sure all QuickBooks files have the same release number and follow these steps:

1. Open a QuickBooks file.
2. Press the *F2* key to bring up the **Product Information** screen.

3. Read the top line for the release information:

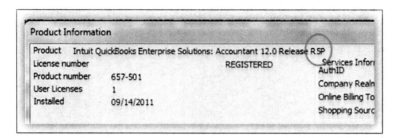

4. If necessary, update QuickBooks by clicking on **Help | Update QuickBooks**.

5. Additionally, you will need to know the file path of each QuickBooks file that you wish to combine. If you do not know the file path, follow these steps:

   ❑ Open any QuickBooks file.

   ❑ Select **File | Open Previous Company**.

   ❑ The submenu contains the full file path for recently opened files. Take a screenshot of, write down, or temporarily memorize this location.

How to do it...

Perform the following steps:

1. Open one QuickBooks file.

2. Select **Reports | Combine Reports From Multiple Companies**.

3. Click on the **Add Files** button, and browse to another QuickBooks file.

4. Fill out the bottom portion of the **Combine Reports From Multiple Companies** screen. Set the reports to select **Date Range**, **Report Basis**, and **Company name**, as shown in the following screenshot:

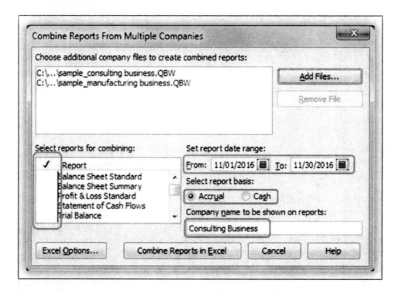

5. Click on the **Excel Options** button for standard Excel settings, such as Freeze Panes, Auto Outline, and the like.
6. Finally, click on the **Combine Reports in Excel** button, and wait while Excel generates these reports from each file, and combines them.

How it works...

The result in Excel is a separate column with the data from each file, followed by a column with the combined figures.

There's more...

If you did not select the **Auto Outline** feature behind the **Excel Options** button, but wish to hide the results from individual companies, then you can hide those columns as follows:

1. Highlight the columns from individual companies.
2. Right-click on any part of the highlighted area.

3. Select **Hide** as shown in the following screenshot:

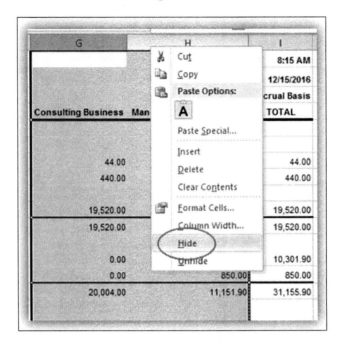

4. Alternatively, instead of right-clicking and selecting **Hide**, click **Data | Group** (Excel 2007 or 2010) or select **Data | Group & Outline | Group** (Excel 2003 or prior). This tool provides greater flexibility in showing and hiding the results from individual company files quickly.

Setting up reports for optimal exporting

Most QuickBooks experts are already familiar with the ability of the software to export to Excel. However, some customizations may be needed in the Excel environment. This recipe includes a tool to eliminate repetitive structural customizations every time a report is exported to Excel.

Getting ready

Perform the following steps:

1. Create a report in QuickBooks, click on the **Excel** button, and then select **Create New Worksheet**.

2. Click on the **Advanced** button.

How to do it...

Perform the following steps:

1. Make your selections on the **Advanced Excel Options** pop-up box. The following screenshot represents my favorite export settings:

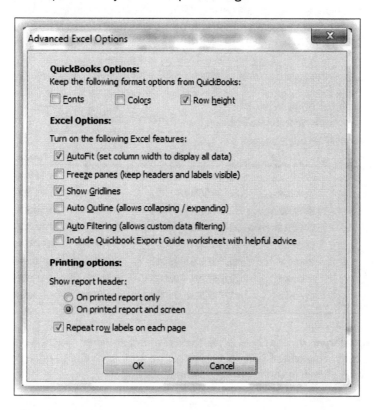

2. Click on **OK**. Please note that these options need to be set only once. The next time you export a report from QuickBooks to Excel, these settings will be present automatically, and there will not be any need to click on the **Advanced** button.

How it works...

We have the following options in Excel that facilitate our working:

▶ **Freeze panes**: If a report is exceptionally long or exceptionally wide, the **Freeze Panes** setting automatically positions the top and/or left margins of the report in the right place, so you do not have to do it manually once in Excel. In the following example, the first four rows and first two columns are frozen. No matter how far you scroll down, the frozen rows are always visible, as shown in the following screenshot:

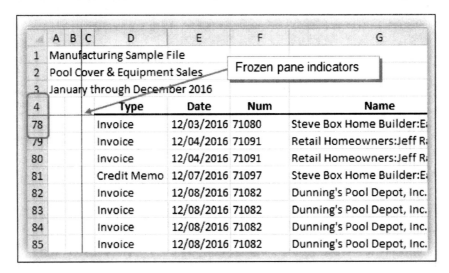

▶ **Show gridlines**: Unless Excel is set to print them, gridlines function only as on-screen visual cues. This option has no relation to the print setting, but only the on-screen setting, as shown in the following screenshot:

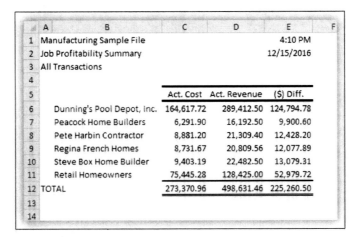

- **Auto outline**: This activates the **Group & Outline** feature of Excel. If the report has columns and subcolumns (for example, a profit and loss report, organized by class, where subclasses exist), then the **Group & Outline** feature gets activated, making it easy for you to collapse and expand subclass columns in Excel. If the report has accounts and subaccounts, customers and jobs, items and subitems, or other hierarchy, then the **Group & Outline** feature activates in the exported report, making it easy for you to collapse and expand rows in Excel, as shown in the following screenshot:

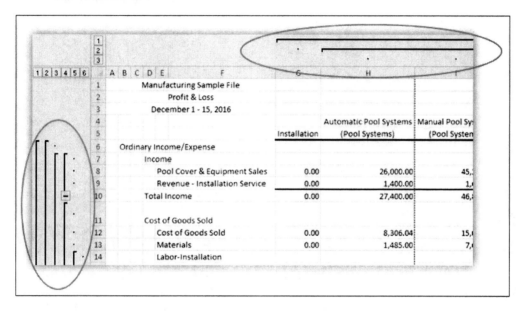

- **Auto filtering**: Being ideal for detailed reports, this option simply turns on the **Auto Filter** feature in Excel, as shown in the following screenshot:

Date	Num	Name	Mem
02/12/2016	71058	Dunning's Pool Depot, Inc.:Angel C	POWERTRAK-2
02/15/2016	71052	Regina French Homes:Wrong Way	Pool Cover, Fo
02/15/2016	71052	Regina French Homes:Wrong Way	ULTIMATE 3000
02/28/2016	71055	Retail Homeowners:Kirby Freemar	Pool Cover - Da
02/28/2016	71055	Retail Homeowners:Kirby Freemar	POWERTRAK-2
03/05/2016	71059	Retail Homeowners:Karen Dee	Pool Cover, Aq
03/05/2016	71059	Retail Homeowners:Karen Dee	ULTIMATE 3000
03/12/2016	RMA71096	Retail Homeowners:Karen Dee	Pool Cover, Aq
03/19/2016	71098	Retail Homeowners:Karen Dee	Pool Cover, Aq
04/15/2016	71062	Retail Homeowners:Marie Gibbs	Pool Cover - Da
04/15/2016	71062	Retail Homeowners:Marie Gibbs	POWERTRAK-2

- ▶ **Show report header**: This option controls whether the report header appears in the spreadsheet cells or in the **Header** section of the spreadsheet, normally accessed through the **Page Layout** feature or **Insert** tab, as shown in the following screenshot:

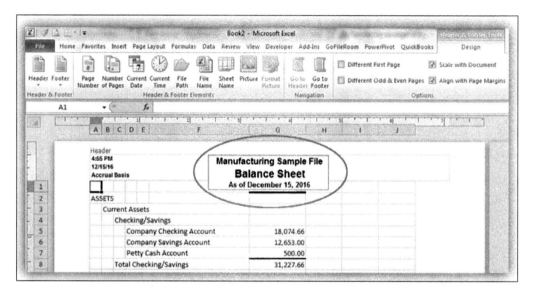

Updating exported reports

Starting with the 12.0 edition, reports already exported from QuickBooks to Excel may be updated when the data changes. This recipe highlights the technique that saves a significant amount of time when Excel reports are customized after being exported. But, when reports are customized, the QuickBooks data changes and the report needs to be updated.

Getting ready

Perform the following steps:

1. Export a report to Excel. Save the report.
2. Customize the report in Excel by changing formatting and row headers, or adding formulas in a separate column.
3. Change or add a transaction in QuickBooks, and refresh the report within QuickBooks.

How to do it...

We have to perform the following steps:

1. Click on the **Excel** button, followed by **Update an existing worksheet**.

2. Browse to the saved file, and then select the appropriate sheet tab from the drop-down list, as shown in the following screenshot:

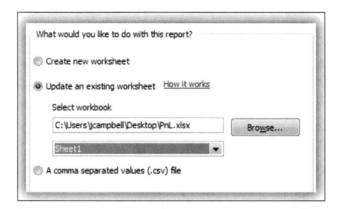

3. Any number of error messages may appear in both QuickBooks and Excel, including the one shown in the following screenshot (with recommended responses):

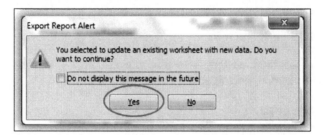

4. The following error message may also come from QuickBooks:

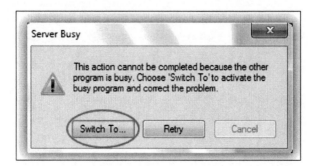

5. The preceding message generally indicates that a separate message is open in Excel, waiting for a response, as shown in the following screenshot:

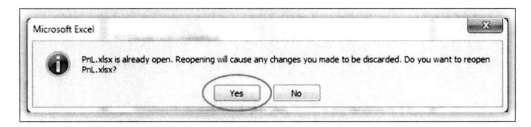

6. When the Excel file is updated, a new sheet is added with the fully updated report, while the previous tab is copied, so that the original remains intact. Delete the original tab.

How it works...

The following changes to the Excel report are preserved while the report is updated from QuickBooks:

▸ Change in fonts in row and column headers

▸ Addition of formulas alongside the report data

▸ Renaming of report titles and column or row headers

▸ Resizing of columns

▸ Insertion of columns and rows

For the most efficient workflow, customize fonts in QuickBooks before exporting, by clicking on the **Customize Report** button, and selecting **Fonts & Numbers**.

There's more...

After the initial export to Excel, a **QuickBooks** tab is added to the Excel ribbon, bearing an **Update Report** button.

This is an alternative method of updating an Excel report with new QuickBooks data, as shown in the following screenshot:

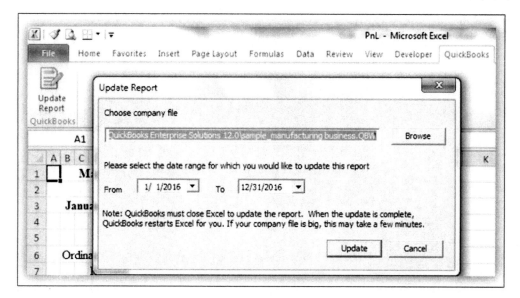

When this button is used for the first time for a given QuickBooks file, the QuickBooks file needs to be open. After that, it is not necessary to open the QuickBooks file.

Using Excel to edit lists hyperefficiently

It is now possible to use a spreadsheet-like tool to manage customer, vendor, and item lists efficiently. Instead of creating or editing one list member at a time (by opening each one, performing data entry, and closing it), the process in this recipe is quite simplified.

Getting ready

From the **Lists** menu, select **Add/Edit Multiple List Entries**.

How to do it...

1. From the **List** drop-down box, select the appropriate list, as shown in the following screenshot:

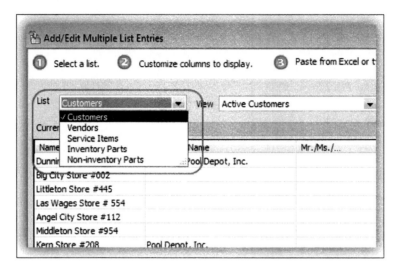

2. Select any item in the list. Then, right-click on any one of the column headers and select **Customize Columns**. Alternatively, select **Edit | Customize Columns**.

3. Display the relevant columns and arrange them in the desired order, using the buttons shown in the following screenshot:

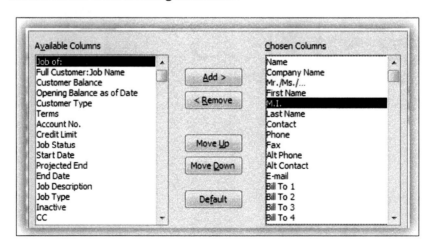

4. After clicking on **OK**, edit the information in the cells through data entry or by copying and pasting from Excel or another spreadsheet, if applicable.

There's more...

Excel includes many capabilities for manipulating data, including text data. The examples include converting names to proper case, standardizing the format of all telephone numbers, or increasing all inventory prices by 5%.

To use Excel functionality in a list, perform the following steps:

1. Export the report to Excel (select **Reports | Lists**).
2. Edit the information using Excel formulas and tools.
3. Use the **Add/Edit Multiple List Entries** feature to copy and paste the updated information from Excel back into QuickBooks.

Some of the most useful functions and tools of Excel for editing lists are as follows:

Functions: PROPER, UPPER, CONCATENATE, LEFT, RIGHT

Tools: Find & Replace, Paste Values, Go To Special, Spelling

11
Supervisory Tools

In this chapter, we will cover the following recipes:

- ▶ Using memorized reports for supervisory activities
- ▶ Creating customized item-based reports to detect errors
- ▶ Detecting errors with standard reports
- ▶ Using the Attached Documents feature to spot-check transactions
- ▶ Using the Audit Trail feature to gather supervisory intelligence

Introduction

This chapter includes recipes for accountants in a supervisory or reviewer role. The reader will be able to locate and address incorrect entries and inconsistencies in the accounting records, by using the latest tools, as well as by using old tools in new ways.

Using memorized reports for supervisory activities

The **Memorized Reports** feature, especially when combined with the ability to customize reports, is a powerful and convenient tool for supervisors and reviewers to quickly focus on key information, and to bring errors to light.

Getting ready

Prepare key reports (recommendations provided in other recipes in this chapter), and add them to the **Memorized Report** list by clicking the **Memorize** button (*Ctrl+M*).

How to do it...

1. Go to **Reports | Memorized Reports | Memorized Reports List**.

2. Click on the **Memorized Report** button, followed by **New Group**.

3. Create a report group named `Error-Checking Reports,` or `Daily Reports,` or `"[Your Name Here]'s Reports"`, or some other distinctive name.

4. Group the memorized reports under this heading.

5. Repeat as desired for various report groups.

6. To run these reports in batches, either click on **Reports | Process Multiple Report Groups**, or double-click on the memorized report header, and then work your way through the **Process Multiple Reports** pop-up window:

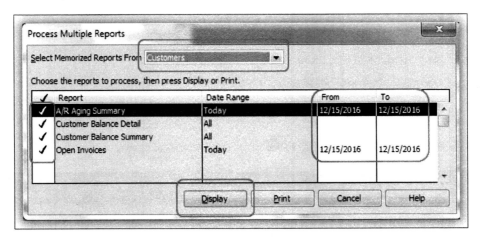

7. Use these reports for your supervisory activities.

How it works...

The **Memorized Reports** and **Process Multiple Reports** features, when used for supervisory work, have two major advantages:

1. Since some key reports may entail significant customization, there is no need to prepare those customizations each time you run the reports.

2. The memorized report groups can serve as a checklist, potentially eliminating the need for additional files and reminder cues in the work environment.

There's more...

Consider grouping the memorized reports based on how you plan on running those reports, for example, by time period:

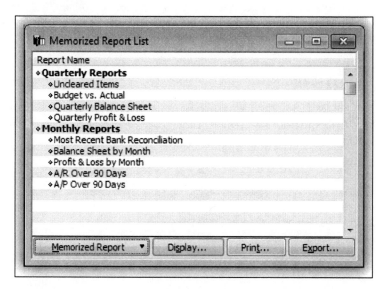

or by purpose:

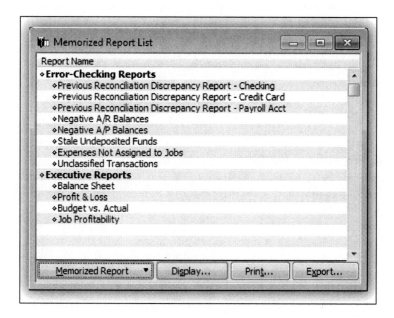

Creating customized item-based reports to detect errors

Depending on the nature of your business, items may be used in unusual ways to detect specific errors. This recipe focuses on the reimbursed expenses or other pass-through charges between you and your customers or independent contractors.

Getting ready

1. Create items for reimbursed expenses or other pass-through charges. Be sure to link them to the appropriate General Ledger accounts. These accounts need not be identical for both the original and the reimbursed transaction:

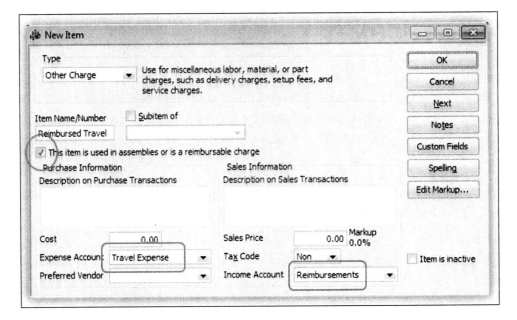

2. Use items to record both the outbound and the inbound transactions, even if you normally wouldn't use items for that transaction. For example, if you don't use the **Invoice** feature and you usually just record a deposit, then use the **Sales Receipt** screen instead:

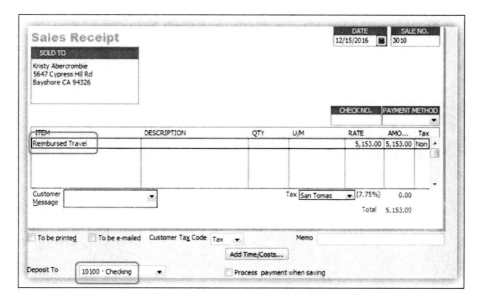

3. When you pay the expenditure, also use the **Items** field:

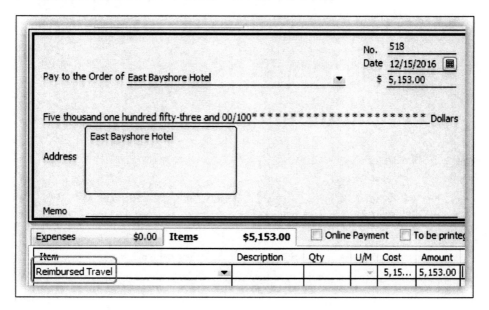

How to do it...

1. Go to **Reports | Jobs, Time, & Mileage | Item Profitability**.
2. Select **Customize Report | Filters**.
3. Set **Choose Filter** to isolate only the items used for these reimbursed or pass-through expenses.
4. Then, select **Header/Footer | Report Title = Pass-through Transactions** or **Reimbursed Expenses**.

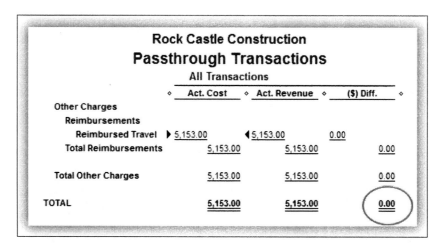

5. Review the **($) Diff**. column; it should be zero.
6. Investigate and resolve all non-zero balances.

How it works...

This report works regardless of the income, expense, or balance sheet accounts used, but focuses purely on the critical information: the ins and outs of a pass-through transaction.

There are several methods for setting up easy ways to isolate the pass-through-related items. One method is to select an **Item Type**, such as **Other Charge**, and use this **Item Type** exclusively for these transactions. If you choose this method, filter the **Item profitability report**, by setting the **Item filter** to **All Other Charge Items**.

Another method is to create one item called **Reimbursements**, and create more specific sub-items, which are account-related such as **Reimbursed Travel**, customer-related such as **Retail Customers**, or vendor-related, such as the names of each individual independent contractor with whom you have reimbursement or withholding arrangements.

In this case, apply the **Item** filter, and select the parent item, for example, **Reimbursements**. All sub items are automatically included in the report.

The result of this method is illustrated in the previous screenshot.

There's more...

As an expert user, you might be wondering why this is advantageous, given the **Billable Expense** feature and the available **Unbilled Expenses** report to catch errors or oversights in the pass-through process.

There are several notable benefits of this recipe over that feature:

 ▶ With the **Items** method, the same procedure can be used regardless of whether the pass-through item comes in first or goes out first.

 ▶ With the **Billable Expense** method, if an invoice is voided or deleted, the **Billed** status of the expenditure does not revert to **Unbilled**. Therefore, since it does not reappear in the **Unbilled Expenses** list, the reimbursement might be overlooked.

Detecting errors with standard reports

Experienced accountants detect errors with some form of variance analysis: a comparative annual balance sheet, a monthly profit and loss. This recipe highlights other methods of detecting errors in the QuickBooks file, which may be otherwise overlooked.

How to do it...

1. **Identify check numbers missing from the sequence**: Select **Reports | Banking | Missing Checks**, and select the checking account:

Rock Castle Construction
Missing Checks
All Transactions

Type	Date	Num	Name	Account	Amount
Check	12/01/2014	93	Reyes Properties	10100 · Checking	-1,200.00
*** Missing numbers here ***					
Check	12/05/2014	95	Express Delivery S...	10100 · Checking	-35.00
*** Missing numbers here ***					
Check	12/10/2014	97	Patton Hardware S...	10100 · Checking	-197.59
*** Missing numbers here ***					
Check	12/20/2014	99	Davis Business As...	10100 · Checking	-2,100.00
*** Missing numbers here ***					
Bill Pmt -Check	01/11/2015	101	East Bayshore Au...	10100 · Checking	-532.97
Check	01/15/2015	102	Bank of Anycity	10100 · Checking	-3,495.82
Check	01/15/2015	103	Federal Treasury	10100 · Checking	-100.00
Check	01/15/2015	104	State Board of Equ...	10100 · Checking	-208.09

2. **Identify transactions altered after being reconciled**: Go to **Reports | Banking | Reconciliation Discrepancy Report**. Modify the columns as indicated in the following screenshot:

Manufacturing Sample File							
Previous Reconciliation Discrepancy Report							
Company Checking Account							
Date	Entered/Last Modified	Last modified by	Num	Name	Reconciled Amount	Type of Change	Effect of Change
Statement Date: 01/31/2016							
01/26/2016	12/15/2016 21:16:08	Admin	5019	Deborah Wood	-10,500.00	Amount	1,000.00
Total 01/31/2016							1,000.00
							1,000.00

3. **Identify altered transactions from a closed period**: Go to **Reports | Accountant & Taxes | Closing Date Exception Report**. This report also displays the closing date history.

Manufacturing Sample File							
Closing Date Exception Report							
Books are currently open							
Entered/Last Modified	Last modified by	State	Date	Name	Account	Debit	Credit
Closing Date History							
Closing date set to 11/30/2016 on 12/15/2015 07:45:24 by Admin							
Closing date set to 11/30/2015 on 12/15/2014 06:47:18 by Admin							
Closing date cleared on 12/15/2014 02:31:48 by Admin							
Closing date set to 11/30/2014 on 12/15/2013 01:24:26 by Admin							
Transactions entered or modified by Admin							
General Journal DEPR1007							
12/15/2016 21:36:23	Admin	Latest	10/31/2016		Depreciation Expense	176.92	
					Accumulated Depreciation		176.92
12/15/2015 07:42:57	Admin	Prior	10/31/2016		Depreciation Expense	76.92	
					Accumulated Depreciation		76.92

4. **Isolate income or expense transactions not assigned a class**: Go to **Reports | Company & Financial | Profit & Loss Unclassified**.

5. **Identify unreimbursed expenses or unwithheld advances**: Select **Reports | Customers & Receivables | Unbilled Costs by Job**.

6. **Isolate expenditures for which the Customer:Job field was left blank**: Select **Reports | Professional Services Reports | Expenses Not Assigned to Projects** or **Reports | Contractor Reports | Expenses Not Assigned to Jobs**.

In the Accountant edition, the menu path for the previous report is **Reports | Industry Specific Reports | Professional Services Reports |** and so on.

7. **Scan for negative inventory quantities**: Go to **Reports | Inventory | Inventory Stock Status by Item**.

Manufacturing Sample File
Inventory Stock Status by Item
December 1 - 15, 2016

	Item Description	Reorder Pt	On Hand	For Assemblies	Available
Inventory					
AN-12x1	Anchor, 12x1 Red...	100	785	500	285
ANAD	Adhesive, Anchor	50	-39	12	-51
ANBA-BL	Anchor Base, Black	100	37	44	-7
ANPI-BL	Anchor Pin, Black	100	36	44	-8
ANSP	Anchor Spring	100	500	600	-100
BO-1/2x4-J	Box, 1/2"x4 Single...	50	18	7	11
CEPE	PED-09-3487 Cen...	100	3	0	3

There's more...

When customizing a report of interest, explore the **Choose Filter** options to create customized reports designed to root out errors and inconsistencies.

Some of the tremendously useful filters overlooked by beginners include the following:

- **Item**
- **Billing Status**
- **Cleared**
- **Entered/Modified**
- **Printed Status**
- **Is Adjustment**

Using the Attached Documents feature to spot-check transactions

This relatively recent addition to QuickBooks is a special form of document management in which source documents are not only stored electronically, but also linked to the transaction recorded in QuickBooks. As a supervisory tool, this recipe includes steps for using this feature to retrieve the stored documents in order to spot-check the way that transactions were recorded.

Getting ready

Make sure that there are source documents scanned and stored using the **Attached Documents** feature.

How to do it...

1. Using the **Find** feature or other means, open up a transaction to which a document has been attached.

2. Identify the transaction as having an attached document by the green paper clip color:

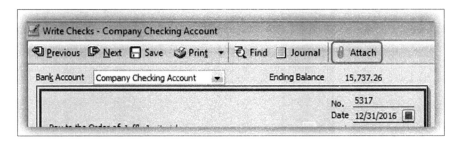

3. Click on the **Attach** button to bring up a list of documents attached to this transaction:

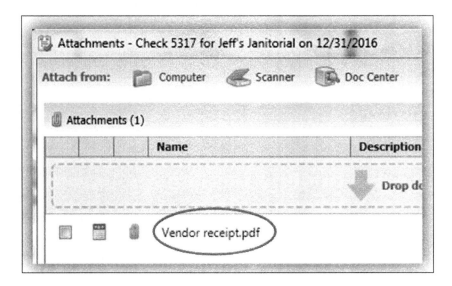

4. Double-click on the document of your choice to view it.

There's more...

The **Attached Documents** feature can include images, PDFs, Outlook e-mails, Excel spreadsheets, and more.

Using the Audit Trail feature to gather supervisory intelligence

The **Audit Trail** feature not only includes the various versions of transactions as they are entered and modified, but also a record of who entered or last modified that transaction–provided that each user has a different login ID and password, which are not shared. Use this recipe to use the audit trail when a supervisory situation arises in which you need to know who was involved in recording a particular transaction, and then speak with that person.

Getting ready

Open a transaction or detail report of interest.

How to do it...

1. If you opened a transaction, then open the **Transaction Journal** (the **Journal** button or *Ctrl+Y*).

2. Select **Customize Report**, and in the **Columns** box, check off **Last Modified By**.

3. At your discretion, also check off **Entered/Last Modified**.

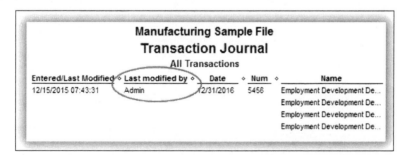

There's more...

Use this feature in your supervisory capacity to talk to the person who performed the data entry about any number of issues, including the following:

- An issue about the transaction
- The circumstances that gave rise to the transaction
- A document related to the transaction
- Customer or vendor relations-related issues
- Authorization surrounding the transaction
- Provide mentoring and support in case of errors
- Investigate concerns about possible fraud

[This feature demonstrates why it is critical that each user have a distinct login ID with a password that is not shared or written down.]

12
New for the 12.0 Edition

In this chapter, we will cover the following recipes:

- ► Refreshing Excel reports
- ► Using Advanced Inventory features
- ► Making a period copy
- ► Using Find & Select during data entry

Introduction

You will be able to use the recipes in this chapter to gain access to the features and capabilities that were not available in previous versions of the QuickBooks Enterprise edition. Recipes for a number of new features are also included throughout this cookbook. Some of these features come with QuickBooks, and some may require additional fees.

Refreshing Excel reports

Except for the Intuit Statement Writer or the more complicated **Open Database Connectivity** (**ODBC**) options, it has not been possible to simply refresh an exported report with the updated information from QuickBooks. The 12.0 edition offers just that opportunity, with little learning curve, and no frills.

Getting ready

1. Run a report in QuickBooks and export it to Excel.

2. Save and close the workbook.

How to do it...

1. Return to the report in QuickBooks, and click on the **Excel** button again.

2. This time, in the drop-down menu, click on **Update Existing Worksheet**.

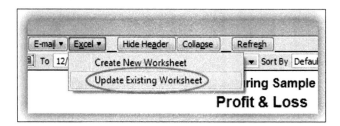

3. Browse to the Excel workbook that you saved in preparation for this recipe, selecting the appropriate tab even if there is only one tab in the workbook.

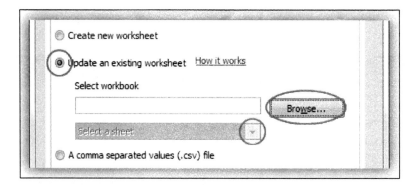

4. The Excel workbook will include a copy of the unchanged spreadsheet as well as the updated report.

Updating from Excel: Alternatively, the ribbon in Excel now includes a **QuickBooks** tab with an **Update** report button.

1. Open the **QuickBooks** file. This step is only required the first time you update an Excel report.

2. Click on the button, pictured in the following screenshot:

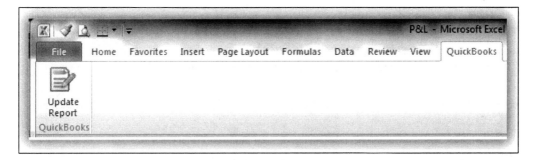

3. Browse to the **QuickBooks** file, and select the desired date range for the report.

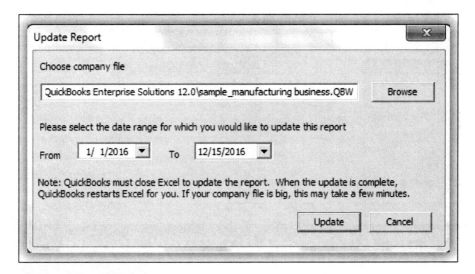

How it works...

Since the update works by sending a new sheet to Excel and changing the name of the old sheet, any formulas on other tabs that refer to the original sheet automatically refer to the new sheet instead.

There's more...

Be sure that the **INTUIT EXCEL ADDIN** application is allowed access to QuickBooks. Do this by selecting **Edit | Preferences | Integrated Applications | Company Preferences**.

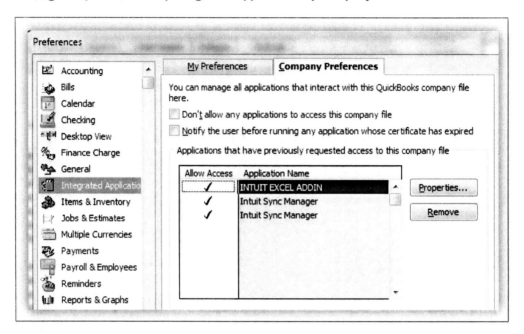

Using the Advanced Inventory features

Features available in this module include the ability to track inventory in multiple locations, use FIFO costing, and tracking inventory by lots. Intuit charges an additional fee for the Advanced Inventory module.

It is essential that the Advanced Inventory features not be confused with Advanced Inventory Receiving. This recipe focuses on the former, which includes FIFO, tracking by series numbers and lots, and multi-location inventory. Later in the recipe we will briefly discuss Advanced Inventory Receiving so the recipe is clear about the differences.

Getting ready

Getting ready for this recipe is more a matter of strategy than preparing the software. The decision-makers in your organization will need to decide whether the benefits of this module are worth the cost, that is, whether the additional business intelligence and reporting features are essential for operations, management, and compliance. This module dramatically expands QuickBooks' usefulness in the inventory space, but many organizations utilize separate, industry-specific software for inventory tracking. Avoid duplication of detailed records; either choose QuickBooks for your detailed inventory reporting or choose your industry-specific software and only enter summary adjustments in QuickBooks.

This recipe is for those who elect to use QuickBooks for detailed inventory management and reporting.

How to do it...

1. Go to **Edit | Preferences | Items & Inventory | Company Preferences**.

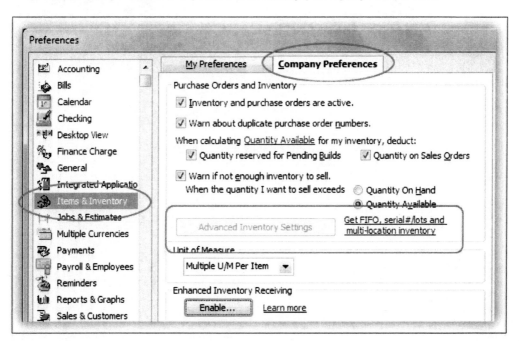

2. Click on the link to begin the process of enabling the advanced inventory features, which at present necessitate an additional cost.

3. Once the features are activated, arrange your preferences for multiple inventory sites.

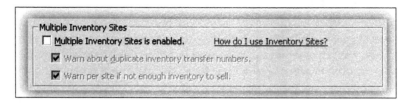

Data entry fields will now include a space for the inventory site, and there will be a separate list for inventory sites, which may include warehouses, distribution centers, trucks, and other sites.

4. To enable inventory tracking by lot or serial numbers, arrange your preferences in the same window.

Note the array of forms for which you may choose to display this information.

5. To set QuickBooks to use the FIFO method of inventory valuation, make your selection in the same **Preferences** window:

6. When creating inventory items, there is now a new button to click on, in order to select the site.

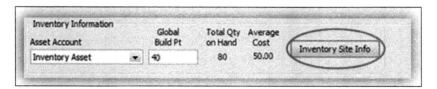

There's more...

Advanced Inventory Receiving, which is different from the previous recipe, is a feature which essentially separates the **Item Receipt** from the **Bill**, using an Inventory Offset account to deal with the received, unbilled items.

The **Advanced Inventory Receiving** feature introduces a small rounding error to the average costing calculation, changes all past transactions upon activation, and requires a purchase order even for non-inventory Parts.

The accounting that occurs using this feature is better reflective of operational practices than accounting principles. But, if your receiving and payables departments are separate, or you experience multiple item receipts or bills, you may want to consider this feature.

To activate **Advanced Inventory Receiving**, select **Edit | Preferences | Items & Inventory | Company Preferences**.

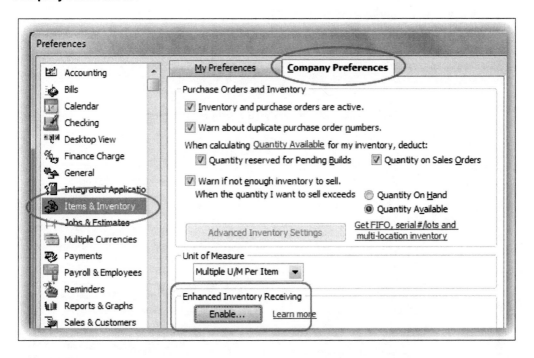

Click on the **Enable** button, and follow the prompts for backing up the file.

Making a period copy

This feature, available only in the Accountant Edition of the 2012 software, is similar to the **Condense Data** utility already available. The main difference is the ability to also condense transactions after a certain date as well, leaving open for detail viewing only a specified period.

Getting ready

To prepare for this recipe, simply make sure that your books and records are complete for the applicable time period.

How to do it...

1. Got to **File | Utilities | Condense Data**.
2. Select transactions outside of a date range.

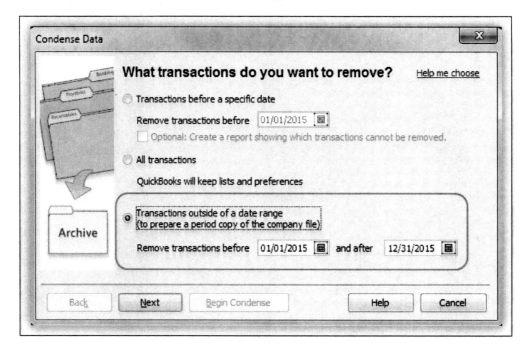

3. Select the range for the dates for which you want to retain the detail in the QuickBooks file.

4. If you are planning to run monthly or quarterly comparative reports for a period which you plan to condense, select the option to create a summary journal entry for each month. Otherwise, select one summary journal entry, in order to preserve opening balances for the uncondensed, detailed period.

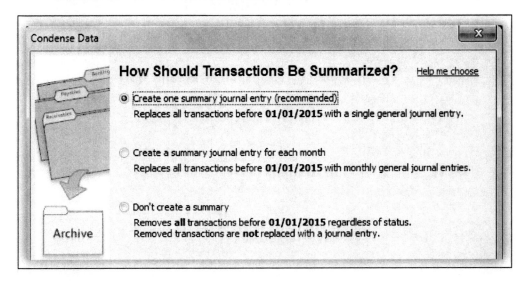

5. Continue to follow the wizard to determine the types of transactions and unused list entries that you want to remove.

6. Follow the prompts to create a backup of the file.

There's more...

The most common reasons to condense a company file include reducing the file size, reducing processing time in daily use, and to prevent outside parties from viewing transaction details upon receiving the file.

This recipe may also be used to create a **Starter Copy**, that is to say, a new copy of the file with all lists intact, but all transactions removed. To use the recipe for that purpose, select **All** transactions, instead of transactions outside of a date range.

Using Find & Select during data entry

The 12.0 version of the Enterprise edition helps the users to quickly find items in the list even without remembering the item code or exact name. This recipe includes instructions for taking advantage of this feature, which is essentially an extension of the **Find** feature in the **Items** list.

Getting ready

Be sure that you have already entered a number of items into your **Items** List. The item types do not matter for the purposes of this recipe.

Open a data entry screen of your choice, which includes a drop-down list for items.

How to do it...

1. Choose **Find & Select Items,** which appears at the top of the drop-down list:

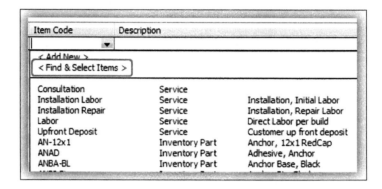

2. From the drop-down box, select the field containing the information that you recall about the item. Type that information into the **Find** field.

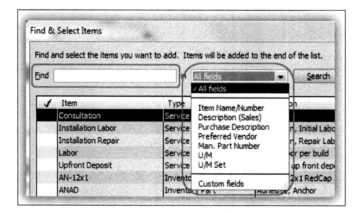

3. Click on the **Search** button.

4. Optional: Check off the desired items in the list and click on **Add Selected Items**. This adds the checked-off items to the data entry screen already open.

Index

memorized reports, using 177-179
supervisory intelligence
gathering, audit trail feature used 187, 188

T

tab 161
Template Name field 108
Templates button 108
Time & Expenses feature 48
To field 67
tools 175
transaction journal (Ctrl + Y) 29
transaction journal report
running 55
uses 55
transactions
Ctrl key shortcuts, using 148-150
memorizing, for assisted entry 91, 92
memorizing, for automatic entry 88-91
spot-checking, attached documents feature
used 185-187

U

Unbilled Expenses report 183
unbilled items
capturing 70
capturing, steps 71-76
uncategorized expenses
classifying 139-141

uncategorized income
classifying 139-141
unclassified transactions
classifying 135-137
uncleared transactions report
about 69
creating, steps 69
variations 70
undeposited funds
about 122
clearing 122, 123
unearned income by customer report
creating 64
creating, steps 64-66
Update Report button 172
user permissions
customizing 7
customizing, steps 8, 9

V

vendor histories
extracting 57-59
View Permissions button 10, 116

W

window
edit customer window 112
preferences window 98

Thank you for buying
Intuit QuickBooks Enterprise Edition 12.0
Cookbook for Experts

About Packt Publishing

Packt, pronounced 'packed', published its first book "*Mastering phpMyAdmin for Effective MySQL Management*" in April 2004 and subsequently continued to specialize in publishing highly focused books on specific technologies and solutions.

Our books and publications share the experiences of your fellow IT professionals in adapting and customizing today's systems, applications, and frameworks. Our solution-based books give you the knowledge and power to customize the software and technologies you're using to get the job done. Packt books are more specific and less general than the IT books you have seen in the past. Our unique business model allows us to bring you more focused information, giving you more of what you need to know, and less of what you don't.

Packt is a modern, yet unique publishing company, which focuses on producing quality, cutting-edge books for communities of developers, administrators, and newbies alike. For more information, please visit our website: www.PacktPub.com.

About Packt Enterprise

In 2010, Packt launched two new brands, Packt Enterprise and Packt Open Source, in order to continue its focus on specialization. This book is part of the Packt Enterprise brand, home to books published on enterprise software – software created by major vendors, including (but not limited to) IBM, Microsoft and Oracle, often for use in other corporations. Its titles will offer information relevant to a range of users of this software, including administrators, developers, architects, and end users.

Writing for Packt

We welcome all inquiries from people who are interested in authoring. Book proposals should be sent to author@packtpub.com. If your book idea is still at an early stage and you would like to discuss it first before writing a formal book proposal, contact us; one of our commissioning editors will get in touch with you.

We're not just looking for published authors; if you have strong technical skills but no writing experience, our experienced editors can help you develop a writing career, or simply get some additional reward for your expertise.

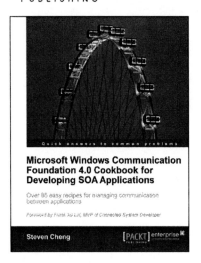

Microsoft Windows Communication Foundation 4.0 Cookbook for Developing SOA Applications

ISBN: 978-1-84968-076-9   Paperback: 316 pages

Over 85 easy recipes for managing communication between applications

1. Master WCF concepts and implement them in real-world environments

2. An example-packed guide with clear explanations and screenshots to enable communication between applications and services and make robust SOA applications

3. Resolve frequently encountered issues effectively with simple and handy recipe

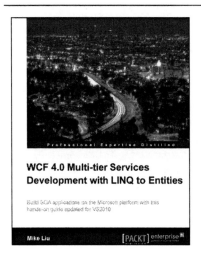

WCF 4.0 Multi-tier Services Development with LINQ to Entities

ISBN: 978-1-849681-14-8   Paperback: 348 pages

Build SOA applications on the Microsoft platform with this hands-on guide updated for VS2010

1. Master WCF and LINQ to Entities concepts by completing practical examples and applying them to your real-world assignments

2. The first and only book to combine WCF and LINQ to Entities in a multi-tier real-world WCF service

3. Ideal for beginners who want to build scalable, powerful, easy-to-maintain WCF services

Please check **www.PacktPub.com** for information on our titles

Expert Cube Development with Microsoft SQL Server 2008 Analysis Services

ISBN: 978-1-847197-22-1   Paperback: 360 pages

Design and implement fast, scalable, and maintainable cubes

1. A real-world guide to designing cubes with Analysis Services 2008

2. Model dimensions and measure groups in BI Development Studio

3. Implement security, drill-through, and MDX calculations

4. Learn how to deploy, monitor, and performance-tune your cube

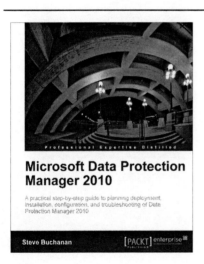

Microsoft Data Protection Manager 2010

ISBN: 978-1-84968-202-2   Paperback: 360 pages

A practical step-by-step guide to planning deployment, installation, configuration, and troubleshooting of Data Protection Manager 2010

1. A step-by-step guide to backing up your business data using Microsoft Data Protection Manager 2010 in this practical

2. Discover how to back up and restore Microsoft applications that are critical in many of today's businesses

3. Understand the various components and features of Data Protection Manager 2010

Please check **www.PacktPub.com** for information on our titles

CPSIA information can be obtained at www.ICGtesting.com
Printed in the USA
LVOW11s1013120713

342615LV00002B/9/P

9 781849 685146